BRITAIN AT WAR

Roger A. Freeman

ARMS AND
ARMOUR

First published in Great Britain in 1990 by Arms and Armour Press, Villiers House, 41–47 Strand, London WC2N 5JE.

Distributed in Australia by Capricorn Link (Australia) Pty. Ltd, P.O. Box 665, Lane Cove, New South Wales 2066.

Designed and edited by DAG Publications Ltd. Designed by David Gibbons; edited by

British Library Cataloguing in Publication Data
Freeman, Roger A. (Roger Anthony, *1928–*
Britain at war.
1. Great Britain. Social life, 1936–1945
941.084
ISBN 1-85409-064-X

Michael Boxall; typeset by Typesetters (Birmingham) Ltd, Warley; camerawork by M&E Reproductions, North Fambridge, Essex; printed and bound in Portugal by Resopal.

Jacket illustrations:
Front, a Civil Defence Warden in Holborn, London; in the background are bomb-damaged buildings. Back, posters adorn Nelson's Column in London's Trafalgar Square. (IWM)

Contents

INTRODUCTION

ALTHOUGH there have been other wars since 1945, many involving British forces, when someone talks about 'the war' there is no question as to which conflict is meant. The Great War of 1914–18 had been 'the war' until 1939, but even those who lived through that earlier grim period were quite willing to have the tag usurped by the later, truly global madness. Second World War may be the officially decreed name, but for anyone who was around, and probably for as many who were not, it is 'The War'.

It was a period during which it seemed that, almost for the first time, the entire nation was shouldering the burden of conducting a mighty, industrialized war and not just the soldiers, sailors and airmen on active service. Civilians died in their tens of thousands, the victims of air raids, while millions more of them gave generously of their time, labour and money to maintain the country's economy on a war footing. As a result the years from 1939 to 1945 have become a demarcation point of this century, dividing it into 'before the war' and 'since the war' – phrases used as commonly by those who were not born until after that event as by those who lived through it.

The following pages, carrying a selection of images, cover what came to be called the Home Front. It was a time of shared dangers and privation for rich and poor alike, when extremes of joy or sorrow reflected public and private moods as the war swung first one way and then the other. There was the stark contrast between the professional's military training and the amateur's defence tactics. The blackouts, rationing, evacuations, bomb shelters, Land Girls, Home Guard, Bevin Boys, endless propaganda, and entertainment are presented in the hope that they will evoke the momentous years of the war, both for those who remember that time and those who regard it as a phase in the lives of their parents or grandparents.

Roger A. Freeman

THE LULL BEFORE THE STORM

To UNDERSTAND the mood of the British people at the outbreak of the Second World War it is necessary to review the effect of the nation's involvement in the previous major conflict, a generation before. The Great War, or – as it became known in the second half of this century – the First World War, had a profound effect upon the morale of the nation. From August 1914 to November 1918, 812,317 UK servicemen lost their lives and 1,849,494 were wounded, mostly on the Western Front in France. By Armistice Day there were few families untouched by grief.

During the years that followed, jingoism was muted and a majority of those who had experience, or knew the facts, believed that repetition of such lunacy should be avoided at any cost. While there was no great embracing of pacifism there was a large-scale turning away from the military, and it was assumed other contestants in the slaughter of 1914–18, particularly France and Germany, were similarly inspired. But in Germany, a defeated and destitute country, there arose a leader who set about restoring national pride. That they became saddled with a dictatorship was of no great concern to the average German citizen experiencing stability and economic progress once again.

Adolf Hitler and his Nazis set out to re-establish Germany as a major European power, backed by the threat of military might. The governments of Britain and France initially did little to meet this threat, believing that even the vociferous Hitler would wish to avoid another conflict. Appeasement became the Allies' mode of diplomacy and what steps were taken to re-arm were neither urgent nor sufficient. The memories of 1914–18 persisted; a repetition was to be avoided.

German investment in matters military during the 1930s promoted the technical advancement that in many areas remained ahead of the British until the final year of hostilities. As a result, on 1 September 1939, when Germany invaded Poland, bringing Britain and France to declare war two days later to honour their commitment to the assailed nation, the Ger-

man forces were better equipped, better trained and better led than the Allies. Morale being an important factor, the British public were not fully apprised of the enemy's capabilities for the authorities themselves were not fully cognizant of the extent of this superiority.

With the declaration of war an overall tension pervaded the British nation. The Press had conditioned people to expect the worst, with devastating air raids and gas attacks a possibility within hours of the commencement of hostilities. The mood was black. However, it was the Royal Air Force bombers that struck first when Blenheims and Wellingtons set out from East Anglian airfields to attack German naval forces near Wilhelmshaven and Kiel on 4 September. The raid proved a costly lesson in how effective the enemy defenders were and how ineffective our bombing. Of the sixteen aircraft that reached their targets, seven never returned. RAF Fighter Command too was to have a painful and embarrassing experience when, two days later, during an air raid alert, two Spitfires shot down two Hurricanes near Ipswich.

Soon the populace took a less serious view of the war for nothing seemed to be happening. Indeed, there was no violation of our mainland airspace by the Luftwaffe. With national tension easing, some of the million and a half evacuees, children and nursing mothers who had been removed from the cities at the outbreak of war, drifted back to their home street environment and the fish and chips they missed so much. People conveniently forgot to carry gas masks, distributed prewar, and the identity cards that had been issued under a National Registration Scheme from 29 September.

Apart from the migrations of evacuees, the Home Front differed little from peacetime. It looked as if the war would be a replay of 1914–18 in so far that it would be fought out on the continent, where the French and Germans faced each other in their respective Maginot and Siegfried Lines. To this western front the British Expeditionary Force was dispatched, in the words of the most jingoistic popular song

◄ A newsvendor and a workman discuss the topic of the day at the corner of Horse Guards Avenue and Victoria Embankment, 3 September 1939. The white bands round the tree were a symptom of the 'blackout' that would take hold that evening.

◄ Corrugated steel shelters, the so-called Andersons, being delivered by London North Eastern Railway to Muswell Hill. These shelters had been free to householders in certain districts since early in 1938. They were partly dug-in, the excavated soil being banked on top.

of the time, to 'Hang out the Washing on the Siegfried Line'. This catchy tune issued regularly from household wirelesses in the winter of 1939/40 in company with other ditties of patriotic flavour. Newspapers and cinema newsreels might be given to exaggeration, but the public trusted the BBC and what was heard was deemed the truth. Of course, the news and views dispensed by this august organization were those largely desired by the government which, if not telling untruths, frequently omitted facts that might depress the nation's spirit. There was no hesitation to repeat unverified claims of British combatants.

Propaganda was supposedly only the tool of the enemy, exemplified by broadcasts from a German radio station in English that became popular alternative entertainment in many British homes. The newsreader was soon known by everyone as Lord Haw-Haw, a tag bestowed by a contemptuous *Daily Express* journalist. 'Did you hear what Lord Haw-Haw said? . . .' became a regular talking point in the pubs and there were frequent assertions as to his up-to-the-minute knowledge of things happening in the United Kingdom. In truth these tales were invariably rumour, distortions by someone who had listened, and further distorted in the re-telling, yet they remain a myth oft quoted as fact to this day. Most people then were too naïve to realize that they were being subjected to psychological warfare.

By the early spring of 1940 the nation had become confident enough for the man and woman in the street to complain about the indignities that war had brought to everyday life. Foremost was the blackout, near total at first but then, when the expected air raids did not materialize, some relaxation was permitted with meagre screened lighting to allow transport to move more safely and a little faster – 25 miles per hour was dangerously fast. During this period the primary task of the Air Raid Warden was to patrol his allotted patch and check for encroachments. The cry of 'Put that light out!' became a music-hall joke. At first the blackout was a deterrent to venturing out at night, but not for long. People might complain but with familiarity came acceptance, if not contempt. The other major civilian moan was rationing. Petrol was the first item to be restricted, with sufficient coupons issued

A roadman's middle-aged wife, an industrious God-fearing woman who kept her humble home spotless, was one of several householders in a Cambridgeshire village who volunteered to take evacuees. She received a young nursing mother and baby from London's East End who, though apparently as poor as herself, shunned domestic chores and neglected hygiene. The cottage woman endured the dirty habits and the regular evening babysitting while her lodger made off to the local pub. However, when she heard that the girl had been seen in a field entertaining a man, this was just too much for her chapel morality. In attempting to admonish the girl her opening remarks were misinterpreted, drawing the cheery interjection: 'Don't know why you're making so much fuss, Luv. I can't fall while I'm still feeding the kid.'

◄ Under the watchful eye of a policewoman, children board a train at Ealing Broadway station to be evacuated to the country. The poverty of the thirties is reflected by two small boys carrying their belongings in pillow-cases.

► Evacuee Freddie King of Bovington Road, Fulham, makes friends with a west country hen.

▼ Many children evacuated from the poorer areas of the large cities had never been to the countryside before. For these small boys from a London County Council Whitechapel School, meeting pigs on a Pembrokeshire farm was a new and exciting experience.

With petrol rationing, introduced at the outset, one could not be choosy about transportation. Mrs Ambrose, wife of the well-known bandleader, and a friend arranged to accept a lift from London with one of her husband's employees. The man, a part-time member of the fire service, had to collect a fire engine for local delivery near to where the Ambroses were living in the country. To his dismay the man found the fire engine was really antiquated; so old, in fact, it not only had open passenger and driver seating, but no windscreen in front of them. To make matters worse it was a very foggy night, made more murky by the blackout. When the man arrived to pick up Mrs Ambrose he apologized for the vehicle not being enclosed as had been expected – Mrs Ambrose being used to travelling in a Rolls-Royce. With no alternative transport and the ladies well wrapped up, they set off at a crawl through unlit streets. After some miles the ladies suggested that the driver stop and wipe the windscreen so they could keep a better lookout for him. In the blackout neither had been able to see that the fire engine had no windscreen. Feeling it would help morale, the driver alighted and pretended to clean the windscreen; a charade he repeated periodically during the long slow journey. Only when they arrived at their destination did he tell the women the facts.

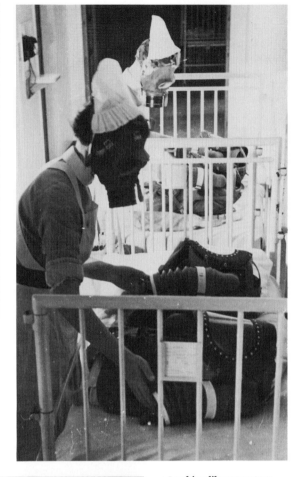

▼ Take your gas mask everywhere you go was the government's decree and for a while the majority complied. As people 'got used' to a war that was not much different from peacetime, carrying gas masks became a nuisance. Eventually few civilians bothered with them. This photograph, taken in The Strand in the first war winter, shows a woman with the familiar square box container holding the standard civilian mask (the state did not supply carrying case) and two men with service-type gas mask haversacks (which the state did supply). Civilians carrying steel helmets usually signified some civil defence duty.

▲ Looking like monsters from another planet, nurses in an infants' ward undergo gas mask drill. The babies were in gasproof containers with concertina air pumps which the nurses had to manipulate. The practicality of baby masks was dubious and, fortunately, they never had to be used in earnest.

▶ Part of the Air Raid Warden's equipment of Percy Tame of Wandsworth, a London office manager. A Civil Defence gas mask, air raid warning whistle, torch and warden's armband. Also shown are the pale blue identity card and ration books issued to all citizens soon after the outbreak of hostilities; the latter issued in expectation of things to come.

The pessimistic forecasts of government departments, echoed by newspapers and periodicals, had conditioned people to expect devastating onslaughts from the air once the nation was at war. In the event, the air raid siren started to wail its warning at Hemel Hempstead just twenty minutes after Neville Chamberlain's solemn announcement on the morning of 3 September 1939. Soon afterwards a farmer's wife, who had told a nervous next door neighbour that her family could use the farmhouse cellar as a shelter, heard a frantic knocking at the door. Opening it, she was confronted by this woman and three children, all wearing their snout-shaped gas masks.

The air raid threat was not readily understood by everyone. Soon after the outbreak of war it was reported to the police at Kettlewell, a village deep in the Yorkshire Dales, that a local woman was not blacking out the windows in the rear of her home, only the front. A policeman was dispatched to inform her that she could be prosecuted for allowing light to show from any window at night. 'Well, tha's daft,' he was informed, emphatically. 'They German aeroplanes'll come from the east. If they want to come to Kettlewell they ain't going to come from Skipton way!'

▲ An item of warden's equipment, issued but never used, was the hand rattle for warning of gas attack.

to allow 200 miles' travel per month for each car.

Following expectations, the war so far was something of an anticlimax for most people on the home front, but it was real enough for those who lived at the ports or who had men at sea. Not only had the feared U-boat attack on shipping materialized, but the first of Hitler's secret weapons had brought additional heavy loss to the merchant fleet in coastal waters. This was the magnetic mine, a baffling device until one was recovered intact from Shoeburyness mud in late November 1939. The Luftwaffe aircraft busy dropping these mines into the sea offshore were the cause of the frequent air raid alarms that sounded inland yet brought no action overhead. Most people had come to look on the wailing siren as no more than a disturbing irritation. The Luftwaffe's harassing of coastal shipping brought the first enemy aircraft down on mainland British soil, a Heinkel He 111 bomber, which arrived in fairly intact condition in a field near Dalkeith, Scotland on 28 October 1939, having been shot down by RAF fighters. It was to be the first of many.

▲ The pullovers and baggy trousers of 1939 give way to army uniform. New recruits get fitted out at the reception barracks.

◄ Sandbags, small hessian sacks that held about one hundredweight of sand, were another common feature of wartime Britain. The manager of this London restaurant let his enthusiasm get the better of him in protecting his premises against blast – and this in the first week of war.

THE THREAT OF INVASION

IF THE NATION had a laid back attitude to the war in the first few months of 1940, it was quickly brought to its senses by the catastrophic events of the spring. Having successfully moved into Denmark and Norway in April, Hitler's army struck west on 10 May through the wooded Ardennes area and swept towards the Channel coast. The French and British forces were no match for the better equipment and tactics of the Wehrmacht. Paris fell in five weeks and within another it was all but over. Hitler had secured the western seaboard of continental Europe from the northern tip of Norway to the Spanish border and only the natural barrier of the sea halted the onrush of *Blitzkrieg*, the lightning war. For the British there was one hopeful outcome of this débâcle.

The crisis of early May saw the charismatic Churchill replace Chamberlain as Britain's leader, but in a matter of days the situation in France was beyond retrieve and with most survivors of the British, and some French forces, backed up around Dunkirk, a sea evacuation was staged. To take the troops off the beaches and convey them over the shallows to naval vessels standing offshore, a fleet of small low-draft powered boats was required. With the urgency of the situation anyone who had a seaworthy, motor-propelled boat was contacted and asked to cross to Dunkirk. The response was amazing; yachts, cruisers, launches, lifeboats, ferries and even paddle-steamers; in total some 700, many manned by weekend sailors, set off – near a hundred to fall victim to Luftwaffe bombs and bullets. Approximately 340,000 men, a third French, were rescued from Dunkirk and brought safely to Kent ports.

It did not need the government to warn the people of the threat of invasion. The general apprehension brought a new willingness to help, a greater sense of national unity. In May recruitment for a part-time militia began, en-

▼ Destroyers bringing survivors of the British Expeditionary Force into Dover from the beaches of Dunkirk. Most soldiers came home with no more than the clothes they were wearing and their steel helmets.

▲ A Hertfordshire Home Guard patrol passes a local pub. A rota required men to report on specific nights of the week and at weekends for duties.

◄ Members of the Springfield, Essex, Home Guard on parade. Being in a likely invasion area these men were early recipients of American-made rifles. Veterans of the First World War were usually given rank with 'stripes'.

► Grandad's Army. John Markham, aged 65, Home Guard at Holy Island, Northumberland, was also a fisherman and cox of the local lifeboat.

The Home Guard was not without incidents worthy of the Dad's Army parody. Weapon training was often conducted by regular army personnel. At one army range in eastern Scotland a Home Guard company was given instruction on the correct way to throw a Mills hand-grenade using live ordnance. For safety reasons the instructor took six men at a time into the trench while the rest of the company watched from a safe distance. Leading round from the throwing bay was a covered dugout in which the six trainees sheltered, to be called out individually by the instructor to take their turn at throwing. Thus, if there were an accident, only the instructor and his pupil were in the bay. When called, each Home Guard would receive verbal instruction from the army sergeant on holding the grenade in the right hand with fingers securing the arming lever, pulling the pin securing this lever with the left and then swinging the right arm back and over, pitching the grenade over the top of the trench parapet, much in the manner of delivering a cricket ball. The four seconds' delay in arming allowed the missile to reach its target about 25 yards away before exploding. Towards the end of the morning, when perhaps thirty men had thrown live grenades, the army sergeant was probably less attentive and failed to notice in time that one rather sullen individual who emerged to 'have a go' was wearing khaki mittens. Having given instruction and the order 'Throw!', the sergeant was horrified to see that the grenade had not left the thrower's hand and was caught up in the wool mitten. One glimpse of his pupil desperately flapping his hand back and forth in an effort to dislodge the grenade was enough; the sergeant dived headlong for the shelter, just in time to evade the inevitable explosion and its lethal shrapnel. Picking himself up, he went back into the bay, expecting to find a mutilated body. To his surprise and great relief there stood the man, quite unharmed, looking over the top of the parapet to where the grenade had detonated close by. Apparently oblivious to how close he had been to mortal injury, the man turned to the sergeant and, holding out a bare right hand, complained, 'Ye ken ma mitten? Went wi' the grenade an' been blawn to bits. Ma wife wull be that cross. She only finished knitting it yusterday.'

rolling men between the ages of 17 and 65 who did not already have part-time duty in civil defence. At first known as the Local Defence Volunteers (LDV), they were renamed the Home Guard in July, by which time numbers had swelled to a million and a half. Sufficient equipment could not quickly be found for this huge force, organized into battalions and companies of existing regular army regiments. Their initial LDV and Home Guard armbands were soon replaced by Denims, the fatigue version of the Army's attire, and by mid-1941 by normal army battledress. At first, until shipments of rifles arrived from America and Canada, many companies trained with a collection of impromptu weapons. Those units farthest away from the likely invasion areas were, generally, the last to be equipped with uniforms, weapons and equipment. The main purpose of the Home Guard was to meet the threat of enemy parachute troops, an expected feature of any invasion attempt. Evening training sessions and nightly duties guarding railways, bridges, factories and other important installations in the locality was the Home Guard's lot. The efficiency of units varied from district to district. Commanders were mostly ex-army officers of the earlier war. Many Home Guard battalions were as efficient in their duties as the hastily trained regular soldiers that appeared in the invasion risk areas.

Practically every vacant country mansion and surrounding park was commandeered for military camps. Often the transports used by these fledgling units were commandeered butcher, baker and grocer vans, still bearing the names of their original owners. Trenches were dug around many of these camps and at good defensive points beside surrounding roads. Concrete pillboxes were built along the planned defensive chains that stretched across England; hexagonal structures that remain the most prominent surviving landmarks of those times. Road blocks and tank traps were set up and large fields festooned with poles and wire, spaced to deter gliders from landing. The familiar white signposts were removed from road junctions, as elsewhere were place names from stations. The British were not going to make it easy for the enemy to find his way through their convoluted road system. Actually, this move would, in the course of the next five years, create more trouble and cost to our own war effort through drivers becoming lost, than ever it could have hindered the enemy had he arrived. Soldiers were everywhere, training intensified and people were on edge waiting for the ringing of church bells that would signify the dropping of paratroops. Bell ringing was forbidden for any other reason. More than one unfortunate cow moving in the darkness was challenged and shot by a nervous guard. And there were not a few soldier and Home Guard casualties through careless or ignorant handling of weapons and explosives, particularly the 'home-made' Molotov Cocktail, a bottle containing an incendiary mixture.

With the threat of invasion new controls and restrictions were issued. No-go areas were declared along the south-east coast, and beaches, promenades and piers were forbidden to civilians. On 2 June 1940, 47,000 children were evacuated from eighteen coastal towns in East Anglia and the Channel counties, 61 per cent of their total school population. The youngsters were taken off to the Midlands and west by 97 special trains. Two weeks later 120,000 school children were moved from the Greater London area. Despite increasing shortages in the shops, rations and a war situation that looked hopeless, most people still seemed confident in Britain's eventual victory, even if they had not the slightest idea how this could come about. And that despite bad news following on bad news that the Ministry of Information could not mute. Then the belief in victory was reinforced by success. It came in the skies.

▲ Road signs being removed – 'for the duration'.

▶ Even footpath signs were removed and at Springfield, Essex, used to good purpose as anti-glider obstructions in a large meadow.

◀ Cars from the scrapyard served as anti-glider obstacles in some fields.

▲Concrete 'pillboxes' were hastily built and camouflaged at strategic defence points; this one at

Putney Bridge is being disguised as a castellated annexe to the church. One pleasant feature of pre-

war days still endured in the desperate summer of 1940, as evidenced here – the Walls 'Stop-Me-And-

Buy-One' ice cream pedal trike whose operator waits for custom at the kerbside. The posters urge the

buying of National War Bonds.

A party of Royal Engineers was engaged in the tricky task of laying mines on the beach at Clacton-on-Sea as part of the anti-invasion defences. Each mine had to be placed in a shallow excavation and then covered with a thin layer of sand to hide it. During the course of this work the soldiers were amazed to see a man, strolling along the promenade, let his dog run on to the beach. The officer in charge shouted to the man to call the dog off, but the animal refused to obey. Realizing something had to be done immediately, the officer ordered those soldiers who had their rifles at the ready to shoot the dog. Hit by the first round, the dog toppled over on to a concealed mine. The detonation set off several other mines close by, but luckily none of the Royal Engineers was hurt. The dog owner, no doubt seeing what his careless walk had caused, quickly disappeared.

A Home Guard sentry was posted to stop all vehicles and check the users' identities. An army car refused to stop, the two officers inside apparently considering it infra dig *to stop for a Home Guard. There was a shot; one of the officers received a bullet through his arm. The car was brought to an abrupt halt. The Home Guard, noting with satisfaction that his shot had had the desired effect of bringing the car to a halt, shouted, 'That'll learn yer. Next time I shan't fire over yer heads.'*

THE FEW

◄With the invasion threat improvised barriers were erected where an enemy advance could be delayed. Soil-filled wooden barrels would not have caused much trouble to a Panzer waiting to cross this ford at Eynesford, Kent, although they provided great fun for schoolboys. If the worst happened the bridge was to be blown up.

◄Upturned farm carts and builders' trestles were used for this road-block in Northumberland. The enemy was unlikely to land so far north but no possibilities could be disregarded.

WHILE THE LUFTWAFFE had been active against coastal convoys since the early days of hostilities, eight months were to pass before the first civilian casualties in England, when a mine-laying Heinkel He 111 crashed in Victoria Road, Clacton-on-Sea, killing two civilians and injuring 156 late on the night of 3 May 1940. There was thereafter a steady increase in incidents, mostly during darkness. To the civilians it appeared that bombs were being scattered at random, although the German airmen were usually attempting to hit railways, bridges or something they thought they could identify. News of a bombing quickly spread in a locality by word of mouth and the novelty brought many sightseers. The morning after would find a host of boys scouring craters for metal fragments. War souvenirs became a popular hobby and if the authorities did not quickly post a guard on a crashed aircraft it would soon be denuded of ammunition, instruments and anything that hands could lever off. Many a horrified schoolmaster caught his

pupils trading such things as live cannon shells for other equally lethal ordnance.

In July 1940 the Luftwaffe began a campaign of action against Channel ports and shipping with the object of bringing RAF Fighter Command's Hurricanes and Spitfires to battle. Not having achieved the desired attrition, on 13 August all-out daylight assaults were begun against airfields, aircraft factories and radio location stations to intensify the battle. Later in the month the enemy's attention was directed to the fighter airfields in the south-east and, finally, commencing 7 September, against London. The primary object was to destroy RAF Fighter Command in the air and on the ground, for air superiority over south-east England was essential if their cross-Channel invasion were to stand a chance of success.

The claims of aircraft shot down by both sides proved to be exaggerated, not by design but rather because of the confused nature of air fighting. True losses were often half or as much as two-thirds of those claimed. While

►Parents wave as a train-load of children leaves Great Yarmouth station on 2 June 1940. An estimated 61 per cent of the school population left this North Sea port which would become a frequent target for Luftwaffe bombers.

Hawker "Hurricane"

This machine has been giving an excellent account of itself in France against reconnoitring Nazi aircraft. It has a 1,030 h.p. Rolls-Royce "Merlin" engine and a top speed of about 360 m.p.h. with a range of 850 miles. In construction the fuselage is of wood, covered with fabric, and eight machine guns are housed in the wings, four each side, firing outside the airscrew disc. Its span is 40ft. and its length 31ft. 6in. Its wheels retract inwards, and in plan its leading and trailing edges are straight. A further distinguishing feature' is the large radiator placed centrally on the fuselage, under the centre-section of the wing.

Page Eight

Vickers Supermarine "Spitfire"

This all-metal fighter, our fastest, has already given a warm welcome to Nazi raiders. A 1,030 h.p. Rolls-Royce "Merlin" engine gives it an official speed of 367 m.p.h., and you can be sure it can do more than that. The "Spitfire" is of all-metal stressed-skin construction, and from its wings spit eight Browning machine guns. This little terror of the air is 36ft. 10in. in span and 29ft. 11in. long, and climbs to 11,000ft. in just under five minutes. Its rudder is smaller and more elongated than that of the "Hurricane," and its wings more pointed and with a definite curve on the trailing edge.

Page Nine

▶ Aircraft recognition publications became popular with the public as an aid in distinguishing friend from foe.

Spot them in the Air!
PUBLISHED BY THE
DAILY MIRROR
3ᴰ 3ᴰ

▼ The Poling, Sussex site, one of the RDF chain stations, generally known to the public as 'radio location' sites. These were the radar installations that could detect enemy aircraft at altitude up to 120 miles away to give warning of an approaching raid. The larger masts carried the transmitting aerials and the smaller ones were for reception.

the skies of Kent and Sussex saw most of the air battles, the Luftwaffe also spread its attacks over a wide area, with formations from Norway attacking Newcastle and Hull. The general public and the majority of service personnel did not know that Fighter Command's strength was gradually dwindling, the flow of replacement pilots and aircraft barely able to make up for losses.

For those onlookers in the fields and streets, with their eyes turned skywards, it was both a frightening and exhilarating time, unable to tell who was friend or foe in the twisting mêlée of specks and vapour trails high in the summer sky; for while a spiralling sheet of flame and smoke would be acclaimed as 'one of theirs', in fact it was often 'one of ours'. But few who lived and worked below this aerial battlefield did not see some positive evidence of the outcome; be it a fleeing Heinkel or Dornier pursued at low level by a Hurricane or Spitfire, or the yellow parachute supporting a German airman gliding to earth. Since the start of the enemy's aerial onslaught, which became the Battle of Britain, the Luftwaffe had sustained mounting losses instead of the easy victory it had foreseen. After a further trouncing on 15 September, Luftwaffe High Command decided that mass daylight operations were too costly to continue and most bombers were then turned to night raids. Churchill's 'Few', the approximately 1,500 pilots of Fighter Command, had lost nearly a third of their original number since the battle began in July. What is more to their credit in the slim victory achieved is that their Hurricanes and Spitfires were not superior fighting machines to the Messerschmitt Bf 109s with which they duelled, the German type having better armament – cannon – and sighting, as well as possessing superior climb and dive performance. But what the Ministry of Information did not know or tell mattered little; for once in this dreadful war the British had a victory.

On a bright Sunday afternoon in September 1940, 16-year-old Denis Baxter was busily taking his bicycle apart to effect some modification. There had been an air raid warning but Denis, like most Londoners, did not let this interfere with his activities. Presently there was the noise of aircraft high above followed by cracking and tinkling sounds nearby. Realizing that bullet cases from an unseen battle above were falling around, Denis told his sister, who had been sitting on the lawn watching the cycle dismemberment, to take cover indoors. No sooner had the Baxters gone inside than the house was shaken by a series of explosions and windows were shattered. Picking himself up, Denis ran back into the garden. There was a small crater in the middle of the lawn and what was still to be seen of his cycle was in decidedly smaller pieces than before. Needless to say, Denis did not appreciate the Luftwaffe's uninvited helping hand.

Winifred Saunders, a hospital sister at Ide Hill, near Sevenoaks, was pushing her cycle up an incline on the way to work when a stricken German bomber passed overhead. The Battle of Britain was at its height and such events were almost commonplace. As she looked up something fell away from the aircraft. After it had fallen a few hundred feet she saw it to be one of the crew and expected a parachute to blossom at any moment. But there was no trail of silk and arrresting canopy; the figure continued to tumble, arms and legs flailing, until it disappeared from view behind the roadside hedge, followed immediately by a sickening thud. Nurse Saunders had spent the whole war in Kent and was no stranger to enemy action above or around; yet her most haunting memory of those years was that luckless German airman plummeting to his death.

▲Observer Corps posts positioned over the whole country, mostly some ten miles apart, were continually staffed by a volunteer force who reported all aircraft movements by land line to a headquarters. This information proved invaluable to Britain's defences.

▼One Observer Corps post with its plotting table was on the roof of the Ministry of Information building in London.

▲ The pilot of this Dornier Do 17Z sent to attack London docks was riddled with bullets by Hurricane fighters. Three of the 4-man crew were wounded, one critically, but they managed to make a 'belly landing' in a meadow just outside Shoreham, Kent on Sunday 15 September 1940, one of 374 enemy aircraft to fall into this county. Soldiers, Home Guards and Civil Defence personnel look on as the wounded airmen are extracted.

◄ A middle-aged citizen registers surprise as captured Luftwaffe airmen are escorted through a London station. This was on 7 September 1940, the day of the first major bombing of London.

DELUGE OF BOMBS

▲ Firefighters dousing warehouse fires following the opening attack of the Blitz in September 1940. In the foreground a burning lighter is being towed to midstream to remove it from the dockside.

WHEN, on 7 September 1940, German bombers attacked London's Dockland, it appeared that the fears of the previous year were at last realized. Many fires burned out of control and next day a provisional estimate of 1,500 casualties was notified, mostly in the East End. The aerial *Blitzkrieg* had continued through the dark hours. The bombers were back the following night and the next, in fact, for 76 consecutive nights with one exception – 2 November, when bad weather intervened – the 'Blitz' continued. This bombardment killed more than 10,000 people and seriously injured three times that figure. Unsuitable flying conditions often reduced or prevented Luftwaffe attention to the capital during the rest of the winter of 1940/41, giving intermittent nights of peace to the residents.

The German bombers did not neglect provincial towns and cities. In October 1940 the Luftwaffe started to make concentrated raids on centres of war production. The most startling heavy attack was made on Coventry, a Midlands city and a centre of automotive and aviation industry. On the night of 14 November a force of 437 bombers unloaded some 600 tons of bombs, devastating the centre, gutting the cathedral and causing some damage to 21 major factories in the area. The holocaust killed 554 people and seriously injured 865. Over the next six months Bristol, Merseyside, Manchester, Sheffield, Portsmouth, Leicester, Cardiff, Swansea, Clydeside and Hull came in for similar concentrated attacks, varying in their severity. A total of approximately 25,000 tons of bombs descended making more than one and a half million people homeless.

During this period many other towns within the bombers' range were attacked in error or as targets of opportunity, while few villages in the south-east did not receive an occasional sprinkling of bombs. But London continued to be of prime attraction and, while less frequent, the recipient of devastating raids, culminating in the night of 10 May 1941 when 1,436 people were killed, 1,792 seriously injured and an estimated 6,000 with minor injuries, while 150,000 properties were destroyed or damaged to some degree. This, London's heaviest raid, also produced the heaviest casualties of any single air raid on the British Isles.

The German airmen were initially given the dock area of London to bombard and thus the main weight of the early raids fell on the East

◀ A heavy anti-aircraft battery in action. Success was limited as the raiders were unseen in the night sky and attacked at varying altitudes. The gun barrage did have an important effect on morale, even if shell splinters in some areas caused more damage to property than to the Luftwaffe's aircraft.

▶ 'Are we downhearted? No!' Members of a stretcher party the morning after the Luftwaffe provided fireworks. These men regularly risked their lives during raids to bring injured out of bombed buildings. The wartime censor has blacked out the Lambeth tag on the overalls.

End and adjacent working-class areas. Later attacks were directed more at the City and boroughs further west, but the poorer areas of the capital continued to be assailed. The meandering Thames could be located by bomber crews on even the darkest of nights, whereas inland towns were more difficult to find and sometimes places that were not the intended targets were attacked. Precise navigation to Coventry was achieved by tracking a radio beam transmitted from the continent, but British defences learned to 'bend' these on other occasions. Although flares were dropped to illuminate and mark targets, for the most part Luftwaffe night raiders could only release their loads in the general area. To avoid congestion and the risk of collision over the target the individual attacks were spread over many hours. British defences could, at this time, do little to counter the night raids, both anti-aircraft artillery and fighter aircraft only shooting down an average one out of every 350 enemy aircraft participating during the early Blitz period, although the position improved later in 1941 as the airborne radar in night fighters became more reliable.

The way ARP wardens and the various civil defence personnel, mostly volunteers, conducted themselves was nothing short of heroic, particularly the firemen who regularly fought blazes while bombs continued to fall around them. In the heaviest raids a third of the streets in some localities were blocked with gas, water, electricity and telephone services torn up. In such conditions fighting fires and retrieving casualties required supreme effort. The majority of the dead and injured had to be wrested from the smoking, stinking debris of demolished buildings and such was the scale of destruction that the dead could sometimes take weeks to uncover. Most of the casualties were among the 60 per cent of Londoners who chose to remain in their homes and not use air raid shelters – although the percentage was much lower in the more embattled areas. The largest proportion of shelterers, some 27 per cent, used the steel Anderson garden shelter or a specially strengthened position in their home. The rest went to public shelters of some kinds. Legend suggests that most Londoners sheltered in 'the tube', the underground stations, but a survey

◄ On the night of 11 January 1941, a bomb exploded in the ticket hall of Bank underground station. The resulting carnage took days to uncover and a temporary bridge was built over the crater. A total of 111 victims were eventually recovered, although rumour had it that many bodies were never found before the underground mess was bricked up to reinstate station and street.

▼ Blitz victims lying on the Oxford Street pavement – clothes dummies from the John Lewis store which was partly destroyed by bombing.

showed that only four or five per cent sought refuge there on a regular basis. Nevertheless, this amounted to 177,000 on peak nights at the 79 stations fitted with bunks and facilities.

The 'bombed out' eventually totalled near one and a half million at a time when London's population was about nine million. Most went to stay with relatives, and special reception centres were set up to deal with the rest while alternative accommodation was found, usually requisitioned in the outer suburbs. Whether or not one could 'take it' was a matter of individual disposition, but overall those who suffered the Blitz were resilient. Morale may have dipped but soon recovered and in London, which received approximately four-fifths of bombs dropped during the 1940–1 raids, the population appeared to become more steadfast as the months went by. Some observers indicate that in a few provincial towns and cities there was greater confusion and some panic among sections of the population on suffering their first heavy raid, resulting in a considerable exodus into the surrounding countryside. But as in London, after the initial shock, people developed a remarkable resilience. 'We can take it,' was their slogan. After the great raid of 10 May 1941 the Luftwaffe's activities over Britain subsided, the reason being Hitler's preparations to attack the Soviet Union involving the transfer of a large proportion of his bomber fleet to the east. Only a fraction of the Heinkels, Junkers and Dorniers remained in France and the Low Countries to conduct what were considered, in comparison with previous experience, nuisance raids. When the Germans invaded Russia in June 1941 more than 43,000 civilians had been killed in the course of the air raids on the United Kingdom, a casualty figure at that time unsurpassed by any combat force of friend or foe on any front.

◄ Deep under the City the shelterers assembled nightly. The disused section at Aldwych station had the track boarded over to give additional space. Several hundred regularly slept here in safety.

►Community bedroom, London, 12 November 1940. An unused tunnel at Liverpool Street underground station had the track tarmacked over and an elevated bench installed, but many still had to sleep on the floor in the warm if stuffy atmosphere.

►An incendiary bomb explodes in a London street. Weighing 1 kilogram, the phosphorus content burned furiously. Incendiaries were released in clusters so that numbers would ignite simultaneously in the same vicinity to overwhelm firefighters. Fortunately, a large percentage of incendiaries failed to ignite when they struck.

▼Children sleep while mother reads propped up against sandbags in a shelter at Victoria Station on the night of 4 November 1940.

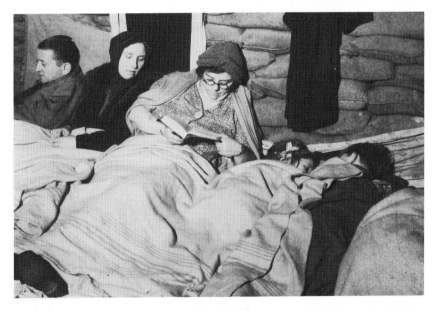

◄ Faces of the Blitz; in a north London shelter an elderly woman has a look of defiance as midnight approaches. Some of the large shelters had film shows and libraries.

▼ Faces of the Blitz; in a Stoke Newington basement shelter, the old chat while a young woman knits and two eat sandwiches. Another woman reads a newspaper with the headline, 'Russia to keep out but ready'.

A 30-year-old motor mechanic from an east coast town was directed to work in a Coventry aircraft engine factory in the summer of 1940. He lodged with a family where both husband and son worked in the same factory, in the same shop and on the same shift. During the Luftwaffe's onslaught of 14–15 November 1940 the three men were among a dozen who took cover in a zig-zag trench in the factory grounds. A direct hit on the trench killed some of the shelterers instantly and buried the rest. Rescuers were only able to extract one man alive, the ex-motor mechanic who suffered only an arm fracture and shock. As hospital facilities were overloaded, after having his arm set the survivor was allowed to go back to his lodgings. He was confronted on the doorstep by his landlady who, for a few seconds, stood looking at him as if in disbelief before her bitterness, sparked by grief, erupted: 'They could only tell me there was one survivor. Why did it have to be you. You're not even a Coventry man!'

▲ A major problem in improvised community shelters was lavatory facilities. Sewers overflowed as in this Stoke Newington shelter where the Shelter Master takes charge.

▶ Safety in 'the tube' was not assured. In a raid on 14 October a bomb smashed through the road to explode in Balham underground station, sending mains water, sewage, soil and rubble cascading down on to the platforms, killing 64 of the 680 people sheltering there. The No. 88 bus never reached Acton Green.

▶ London Warden No. 3260, 60-year-old Henry Burrows, who joined the ARP in September 1940, was soon 'in the thick of it'.

▶ Far right: London Warden No. 3783, Pauline Kettle, a 21-year-old and as smart as they came.

◄ With faces raised towards the almemar, worshippers at the Great Synagogue at Stepney, have praying shawls over their Civil Defence uniforms. 'Tin hats' carry the 'W' identity for Wardens and 'SP' for Stretcher Party bearers and are colour-coded according to grade; the man nearest the camera with a banded helmet is a supervisor. The building was bombed at a later date.

▶ Another specialized Civil Defence duty was that of Fireguard, an on-the-spot watcher with stirrup pump and water bucket. A tricky task, but fireguards saved many buildings by extinguishing small fires before they could get out of control.

◄ No. 10 Downing Street has temporary repairs to its blast damaged windows after bombs dropped nearby in February 1941.

▶ A furniture store engulfed in flames after some 340 Luftwaffe aircraft visited Manchester on 22/23 December 1940, following it up with 225 aircraft the next night.

▶ Far right: An annexe at Buckingham Palace took a direct hit. The morning after, Winston Churchill joined the King and Queen to inspect the damage. The Palace was hit on three separate occasions during the Blitz.

▲ The centre of Coventry blazes, November 1940. Every shop on the right side of the street is either blasted or burnt out.

> Duncan and Andy were having a drink after a hard night fighting fires in Clydeside warehouses. 'Y'ken Andy, A'm thinking hoo the hell are we gang to win the war.'
>
> 'Dinnae be so bloody daft, mon,' Andy scolded, 'of course we'll win. We're the bloody British arrunt we!'

▲Above left: The Blitz on Birmingham. AFS (Auxiliary Fire Service) personnel douse a smoking ruin in Small Brook Street.

▲Dawn highlights the billowing smoke clouds over Swansea. The town was bombed on three consecutive nights in February 1941; 222 people were killed and 254 injured.

◄Firemen work beneath the tram cables as parts of Manchester blaze.

▲ Bombed-out residents leaving Southampton after their third raid, on 1/2 December 1940, which caused much destruction in residential areas and a general shortage of water.

▶ Gas masks in hand, junior citizens of Southampton wait for transportation that will take them to a safer area. Some 180 people were killed and 380 injured in the three raids.

During the early war years rumours were rife concerning spies, saboteurs and fifth columnists, practically all being the result of active imaginations. Nevertheless, the police were warned to investigate all reports of suspicious persons. At Pitchcott, near Aylesbury, the constabulary was told of a man with a suitcase seen late at night on country lanes who suddenly made off across the fields when someone approached. Undoubtedly an enemy agent. The local bobby was sent to investigate and eventually tracked down the suspect. He turned out to be a Liverpool accountant who, after the first heavy raids on the city, had evacuated his wife and children to relations at Pitchcott. At weekends he went to see his family, a difficult journey with many train delays and necessitating a walk of several miles before he eventually reached his destination, often very late at night. The man had discovered that a mile or so could be cut from the journey by taking a short cut across the fields.

◄ Great Yarmouth, on the Norfolk coast, had more than its share of Luftwaffe attention. One of its 60 attacks in 1941 left this dockside warehouse an inferno.

► On the nights of 13/14 and 14/15 March 1941, Clydeside was heavily bombed and a dozen shipyards were damaged. Some bombs fell on tenement buildings, bringing yet another exodus of homeless as seen in many British towns and cities.

◄ Plymouth, with its naval base, was another sea port that came in for ferocious attack. By April 1941 the centre of the town had been gutted.

► Liverpudlians set off for the shops on a fine day in early May 1941. The bomb that took lives and devastated the terraced houses in their street also mangled a car beyond recognition. Liverpool was targetted on several nights over a period of some months.

▼ Work-goers pass the devastation in Fitzalan Square, Sheffield, after the night raid of 12 December 1940, which caused 945 casualties.

A German bomber was brought down near Weldon, Northamptonshire one night in February 1941. The following morning a swarm of children from the neighbourhood arrived at the site to look for souvenirs. Despite the sentries some were successful and 13-year-old Stella Dixon saw a gauntlet flying glove in the dirt which she quickly picked up and put in a coat pocket. Very pleased with herself, she hurriedly cycled home to Corby and proudly produced the find in her pocket for her mother to admire. It was only then that Stella was horrified to see that the glove contained a severed hand. Her mother was even more horrified and alarmed at the thought of the trouble they would be in if the authorities found out. Stella was quickly dispatched with her gruesome trophy and instructions to bury it. The spot chosen was a garden beside the Weldon Road and as far as is known the buried glove and its contents have never been unearthed.

YOU'VE HAD IT!

As REQUISITES of everyday life became scarce, many shopkeepers introduced their own form of rationing for regular customers. This did not stop the customers asking for more and such requests were met with the advice that they had already had their reserve share. 'You've Had It!' eventually became the catchphrase of the Home Front, applied to a variety of negative situations. The housewife who got to the front of the queue for a rabbit just as the last was sold was told 'You've had it, dear.' The unfortunate air raid warden, run down by a bus in the blackout, was also said to have 'had it'.

Rationing may have been the housewife's chief worry and persistent grumble, but the reasons for the restrictions on the amount of food, fuel and clothing an individual could purchase were generally understood and accepted. Its approval by the people rested more with the belief that whether rich or poor it was now share and share alike, rather than a concern to save shipping space. While the wealthy were able to supplement rations with black market purchases or eat in restaurants, this was shrugged off as inevitable and tolerated by the masses so long as the basic system of distribution remained fair. In 1939 Britain imported more than 60 per cent of required foodstuffs; by 1941 this had fallen to under 40 per cent and a year later to 30 per cent. Food rationing had been foreseen and the necessary ration books printed prior to the outbreak of war. They were distributed from November 1939, but it was not until the first week of January 1940 that the procedure was introduced.

The initial foodstuffs to be rationed were butter, sugar and bacon which included ham. Amounts per person were 4 ounces of butter a week, 12 ounces of sugar and 4 ounces of either bacon or ham; this last proved needlessly stringent and was doubled before the end of the first month. Meat was placed on ration in March 1940 and because of the differing value of cuts the amount allowed was decided by price rather than weight. The initial meat ration was one shilling and ten pence worth (equivalent to nine new pence) per person, which averaged a little over one and a quarter pounds in weight. Offal, the waste meat in butchering, was not rationed, nor was poultry, game and fish, all of which went up in price and disappeared 'under the counter'. Following the fall of France, margerine, cooking fats and tea were rationed, the four ounces of margerine or cooking fats being added and linked with the butter ration to allow some flexibility of choice. The limitations on the British 'cuppa' was the hardest blow and the two ounces per person per week curbed the enjoyable habit of many. Although an upsurge in cattle slaughtering allowed the meat rationing to go as high as two shillings and sixpence worth (twelve and a half new pence) during the 1940 Blitz period, it was more than halved, to 14 pence worth (six new pence), early in 1941 when livestock numbers fell dramatically. The screw was really turned during that year, with jams and other tinned and bottled preserves being rationed in March at a pound per person per month allowance. Scanty though the rationing may now appear in the light of present-day eating habits, it is true to say that some families had never fed so well, or had such a balanced diet, until the war years. A young girl from the East End of London evacuated to a family at Sawston, Cambridgeshire, was privileged in that her foster parents had a telephone and her father, a publican, was also on the 'phone. She was overheard when telephoning home to say, 'Daddy, it's lovely. We have "afters" for dinner every day.'

In May the favourite constituent of the packed lunch sandwich, cheese, was an unpopular addition to the growing list, particularly as the ration was only one ounce per week. The outcry from manual workers saw special supplementary cheese for miners and farm men. The following month eggs came under what was termed 'controlled distribution'. There were no ration coupons for these, but retailers had to restrict their registered customers to a share in accordance with supplies. This might be an average one egg per

► A grocer stamps the ration book for the weekly groceries of an RNVR officer's wife, 24-year-old Olive Day of Kensington, in 1941: a four-ounce packet of tea (for two weeks), two ounces of butter, four ounces of margarine, four ounces of bacon, four ounces of cooking fats and eight ounces of sugar.

▲ A common feature of everyday life in wartime Britain was the queue. Bakery produce was not rationed although restriction of supplies meant that particular bakes were only available on certain days of the week. Then it was a case of first come, first served, as at 253 High Street, London NW1.

► Actor Derek De Marney auctions a banana at a Russell Square warfare display. Bananas were rarely seen and this, brought from overseas by an air traveller, appears very small and rather green. Nevertheless, it fetched £5. for charity.

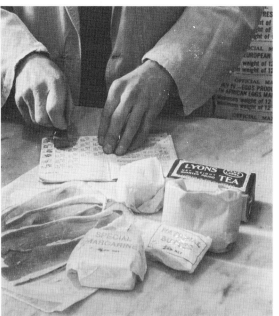

▲ Even royalty had ration books. This is Princess Elizabeth's, issued on 16 January 1940 and showing the meat and cooking fat coupons.

Renee Blain, a 17-year-old nursing auxiliary at St Albans, was detailed to collect the sugar ration for her ward from the foodstore. Her hasty return along the narrow hospital corridors came to an abrupt halt when she rounded a corner and collided with a trolley on which a deceased person was being conveyed to the mortuary. With the impact, sugar cascaded over the covered corpse. Where something as precious as sugar was concerned one could not afford to be squeamish and the understanding porters waited until Renee had brushed the last grain off the shroud back into the container.

week per person, except for priority cases with a doctor's certificate, who could receive one per day if the supply was good.

The next products to be rationed were canned foods – meats, fish, vegetables and fruit – by what was known as a points system. Various products, depending on their assessed food value and weight, required the surrender of differing numbers of points coupons in the ration book. An adult received sixteen points per week and was permitted to save points from one month to the next. Other packaged foodstuffs, not already covered by rationing, were eventually added to the points system, with an increase in the number of points allocated each individual. In July 1942 confectionery, which had already disappeared from view in most shops, came on a new personal ration book with an allowance of two ounces per head, increased to three ounces the fol-

lowing month, per head. Many children did not see a sweet during the latter years of the war, let alone eat one, for while mothers might use the precious points more wisely, it appeared that rationed or not, confectionery disappeared from the shops.

Milk also came under controlled distribution in 1942 and while children, nursing and expectant mothers and doctors' priority cases received a generous pint each day if required, the rest of the population might be rationed by the dairyman to half a pint each day or, at worst, every other day.

With rationing many of the well-known proprietary names began to disappear from packaged foodstuffs. Imported maize for the popular cornflakes breakfast cereal gave way to wheat flakes under the brand name Farmers Glory. Packeted dried powdered egg, available in lieu of shell eggs if required, were considered a last resort by most housewives and then usually only as a constituent of cakes and puddings. Scrambled powdered egg and powdered egg sandwiches were another favourite topic of music-hall jokes, such was their

reckoned unpalatability. For those struggling on a meagre milk ration, National Dried Milk could be purchased in large cylindrical tins. This was equally as unpopular as powdered egg and was most often submerged in coffee or tea.

Bread was not rationed, but in 1942 the generally preferred white loaf finally disappeared. White flour was made by the removal of grain husk and germ, a process resulting in only 70 per cent of the wholewheat becoming

▲ Main portion of the weekly ration for two people, summer 1943. Twenty-eight pence worth of mutton, bacon (8oz.), cheese (2oz.), lard (16oz.), sugar (8oz.), jam (8oz.), chocolate (6oz.) and powdered egg (2oz.). A pint of milk per day was a seasonal boost.

There were remote villages where the impositions of wartime economy were viewed more as a challenge than a necessity of national order and fairness. When confectionery all but disappeared, one enterprising village grocer in the north discovered a large quantity of boxed peppermints at a wholesaler's warehouse. He hurriedly bought all, without asking questions lest the wholesaler's staff suddenly awoke to their scarcity value. The grocer's delight that he would now be able to keep his customers supplied with peppermints for many months was short-lived. On unpacking the purchase in his shop, a more careful perusal of the boxes revealed that Rennies were not peppermints but indigestion tablets. Undaunted, for the rest of the war, Rennies were offered to the villagers as an acceptable substitute for confectionery.

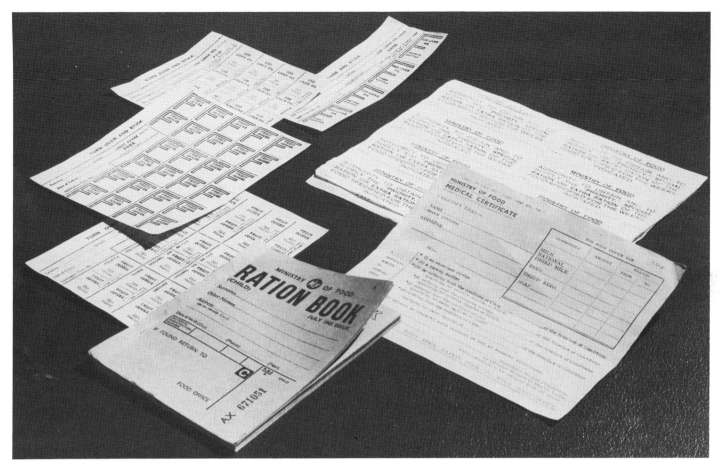

▲Infants were allowed fruit juices and cod liver oil for which special coupons were issued, supplementary to the ration book. A medical certificate (on right) from a doctor, would buy an expectant mother, a nursing mother, or someone suffering from a specified complaint milk (dried or fresh) and soap.

flour. While the husk and germ normally went for animal food, the critical shipping situation decreed that a greater proportion of whole wheat be used for home consumption and the flour extraction rate was increased to some 85 per cent. The resulting flour, of coarser texture, was described as 'grey' looking and the bread it produced was unpopular with most people despite its acknowledged healthgiving characteristics through having greater roughage. However, National Wheatmeal Bread was to be around for many years and eventually people learned to 'get used to it', to use another well-aired saying of the times.

Inevitably there was a black market in food but generally local and on an insignificant scale; it was mostly a case of someone knowing someone who could get a rabbit or a chicken or a dozen eggs from the countryside. Farmers were courted by people who would never have given them a second look in pre-war years. Much of the illicit food from other sources that found its way to civilians came from military pantries where, in practice, rationing was not so severe. A slab of plum

cake smuggled out of the camp under a great-coat could quickly earn you friends in the local community. The vast majority of foodstuffs obtained outside rationing came from people's own efforts to produce background produce. Encouraged by government from the outset of the war through such campaigns, as 'Dig for Victory', allotments flourished and the once neglected flower borders of semi-detached houses grew potatoes and cabbages. The clucks of backyard hens were commonplace and in the most unlikely quarters, while the grunt of a fattening pig was not a rare sound in a suburban street. The contribution of domestic livestock producers was officially encouraged with helpful advice, particularly on how best use could be made of feeding household kitchen scraps and surplus garden vegetables.

To deal immediately with sustenance for the bombed-out, the Ministry of Food organized a 'Flying Food Squad' of mobile canteen vehicles, many of them gifts from the Empire, manned by Ministry of Food employees with the help of the Women's Volunteer Service.

◄There was still room for fashion in wartime Britain and these models were showing off the spring designs for 1941 along the white-edged pavements of Knightsbridge, while window-gazing in Harrods. Decorated hats were still very much in vogue. Hems were just below the knee and suits liberally tailored – rationing yet to descend. The 'sensible' shoes were a gesture towards wartime requirements. The girls also sport the fashionable permed hair styles of the period.

At times the catering for the armed forces was not very precise. In the spring of 1941 a company of Scottish engineers, occupying a country mansion in East Anglia, unexpectedly received a lorry-load of meat which, on assessment, amounted to a complete side of beef per man. Urgent telephone inquiries to neighbouring installations revealed that, while not having such an over-generous supply of meat, they were not in need of more.

Aware of the perishable nature of the acquisition and not having any refrigeration, the unit's officers decided to turn a blind eye to any unofficial disposals the kitchen staff might arrange. As a result, every girl in the local village who was 'walking out' with a soldier returned home at night with a prime joint under her arm. For a week beef was served up in almost every household and beef sandwiches were everyday fare for farm workers. Having exhausted trustworthy civilian outlets the army cooks turned in desperation to the local canine community where, by some unfathomable form of communication, the news spread like lightning. In the parkland surrounding the requisitioned mansion dogs of all shapes and sizes were to be seen making off with enormous cuts of meat. Evidence of this extraordinary feast – large bones – was to be found around the village for years afterwards.

▲ Actress Diana Wynyard, then appearing in *Watch on the Rhine* in London's West End, sits in her flat modelling a brown check suit by Simpsons of Piccadilly, costing £4.12s.6d. and requiring 18 coupons.

◄ A model shows off a white-and-brown striped rayon Atrima utility dress, requiring seven coupons and costing £2.10s. (250 new pence).

Static communal feeding centres were set up in raided areas and these continued to be maintained and increased. Known as British Restaurants, by April 1941 there were 246 in 119 towns. On the following 23 August the 1,000th was opened at Slough by Lord Woolton and the figure doubled again. Serving two-course nutritious and palatable meals at low prices, they were a boon.

Eating out at other establishments became more difficult from 1942 under a series of 'Acquisition of Food Orders' when some meals might involve surrendering personal food coupons. Meals were then compulsorily limited to three courses with a maximum cost of five shillings (25 new pence). Charges for cabaret and service were limited to 3s. (15 pence) and 6d. (2½ pence) respectively. There was a let-out for some night clubs and hotels with a maximum 7s. 6d. (37½ pence) house charge. Restaurants by law had to close at 11 p.m. except in London, the universal leave centre, where they could stay open until midnight.

To avoid the high price rises of the First World War, food was subsidized; £205,800,000 in 1943 alone. By this means food was kept to within 20 per cent of its pre-war price.

Food was only one of the restrictions besetting everyday living. In June 1941 clothes and textile rationing was suddenly introduced, using a points coupon system with 66 points allocated to each adult for a year. The nature and cost of the article determined the coupons required. As examples, a boy's vest in wool/cotton costing 5s. 8d. (28 new pence) needed two coupons; whereas a man's cotton vest at 2s. 3d. (11 new pence) demanded four coupons. While a bra at 2s. 9½d. (15 new pence) only needed a single coupon; a nightdress at 12s. 11d. (65 new pence) required six. Suits, dresses and coats made the biggest inroads into the clothing coupon allowance, requiring anything from ten to sixteen points. Even with rationing, restricted production led to shortages and rising prices so that in the spring of 1942 the ration was reduced to what amounted to 48 coupons per year per person.

At this time the government announced the introduction of 'Utility Clothes'. These were manufactured from a limited range of materials and to specified standards so that good clothing was available to the public at controlled prices. As these garments generally cost substantially less than equivalent articles from uncontrolled production – in some instances as much as a third less – they were immediately popular with the public. Designs were not specified and several well-known fashion houses produced women's suits and dresses within the utility scheme. For example, in the spring of 1943 John Lewis's London store was selling a striking black-red-and-white check wool short dress by Dorville at 75s. (£3.75 in today's money) which required eleven coupons. A scarlet wool frock from the same house designer cost 60s. (£3.00) and required the same number of coupons.

The clothing ration was severe enough for shabbiness to be accepted in even the most august establishments. Patched jackets and trousers were seen in West End clubs and exclusive restaurants. Under the banner of 'Make Do and Mend' the government encouraged the refurbishment of garments and gave out helpful tips. The darns in wool socks were darned again. Old wool sweaters and jumpers were unravelled and knitted into something useful. Many 'best room' curtains finished their days as women's dresses. The shortage of materials made parachute silk a most highly sought item for use as underwear, silk scarves and wedding dresses. Any airman who did not immediately gather up his canopy after successfully baling out was unlikely to see it again. For women who still sought to be fashionable the absence of silk stockings – which had disappeared in 1940 – was the most troubling aspect. In summer weather some girls turned to the bottles of 'liquid stockings' and painted seams up the back of their legs, but this was not popular and easily discerned. One outcome was an increase in the number of women wearing slacks, often fashioned from men's trousers.

Much to the delight of small boys who foresaw relief from washbasin and bath, soap was added to the rations inventory in February 1942 at one pound per person per month. In practice this was quite sufficient for most households, given frugal use, while those persons engaged in very dirty jobs could obtain a supplement. As the months went by there were many household items, once taken for granted, that became scarce and virtually unobtainable; safety-pins, candles, shoelaces, elastic and much else that may not have been essential to life but whose absence could make life difficult. Domestic hardware, pots, pans, kettles, basins, jugs and crockery also became hard to find, although utility pottery was introduced from July 1942. A village emporium in Essex became known as one of the few sources of china chamber-pots and the 'job lot' taken to clear a Blitzed warehouse proved a lucrative investment for this rural entrepreneur. Many articles were either no longer made or only in limited production for a variety of reasons, usually labour and material shortages or the diversion of part of the factory to priority war work.

Surprisingly, petrol, the first commodity to be rationed, continued to be supplied for private motoring until March 1942. Then it was finally recognized as a luxury for which the risking of seamen's lives could no longer be justified and private motoring was banned. Rationing continued for essential business purposes, which still allowed those who qualified to combine business with pleasure within the law. A doctor could drop his wife off to go shopping while he went to the hospital, and

farmers' cars, each with a trailer in tow, could often be seen outside a favourite hostelry on the way back from market.

If the private motorist had laid his car up for the duration there was no decline in the number of petrol tankers seen on British roads. With petrol companies pooling resources, the tankers then all wore grey paintwork and the identification POOL as most busily hauled fuel for the ever-thirsty air forces. There was some promotion of 'producer gas' equipment, notably by public transport. Buses towed small trailers carrying the solid fuel burning apparatus that was exceedingly troublesome. It became the expected thing on some routes for all passengers to dismount and help assist the vehicle up steep gradients by pushing.

Solid fuel was not rationed but subject to controlled distribution with merchants allocat-

▼ Utility became a sign of value for money. Several top designers worked to these requirements, including Norman Hartnell. The 1943 Berkertex design in a West End store were his work, with prices in the £3 range.

ing as they thought fair with the available, fluctuating supplies. In bad winters solid fuel became very scarce and unobtainable for weeks at a time in some areas. Restriction on the use of gas and electricity was requested, but, being difficult to effect, never imposed. Thus the users of these power sources were at a distinct advantage over those, mostly rural dwellers, who could only use solid fuel for heating and cooking. Country folk turned to firewood but this was often unsuitable for use

Every development on the Home Front brought forth appropriate jokes, often crude. Favourite when Utility Clothing made its appearance, if harmless by today's standards would have been far too suggestive for the BBC but not a comedian at a factory concert: 'Have you heard about the utility knickers? One yank and they're down!'

Such was the spirit of the people during the threat of invasion, that many gave voluntarily to the Chancellor of the Exchequer to further the war aims. The Public Purse had some strange credit entries in those years, which the Ministry of Information disclosed to encourage others. Mrs E. Stone of Enville, Stourbridge, to celebrate her birthday on 20 April 1941, sent two shillings and sixpence towards a bomb to drop on Berlin. Customers of the Old Dog & Badger at Maulden in Bedfordshire, sent £12, Gibraltar evacuees in London gave £12 and Master Leslie Talbert, who held a sports meeting among the children of Sanderstead, collected 12 shillings. These are a few examples of thousands of gifts, which also included hundreds of ambulances and mobile canteens.

▲ Utility underwear was practical. The wool vest cost 3s.9d. and three coupons, the panties 3s.6d. (17½ new pence) and three coupons.

▶ Utility furniture; simple, plain, sturdy and good value for money, as it was all built to strict specifications. About £100 furnished this bedroom. Furniture manufacture was banned in summer 1942 with the exception of 22 utility items. As production was limited, newly-weds, the bombed-out and other deserving cases received priority.

in cooking stoves. Britain had relied on imports for a large proportion of timber requirements, now severely curtailed. Fortunately, the country was well wooded and extensive felling ensued. Reasonably priced furniture became a thing of the past following the losses due to air raids and the very limited production that continued in wartime Britain. By 1942 it was apparent that some increase in furniture manufacture must be allowed to meet the growing shortage and this, like clothing, was subject to a Utility Scheme which prescribed materials, qualities and, additionally, designs. If the result was plain and functional, at least the soundness of Utility furniture made it very good value in comparison with the inflated prices being paid for secondhand items. The Utility tag eventually came to most domestic items manufactured in wartime Britain through the specifications laid down by the Board of Trade in what had become a highly controlled economy.

THE SOCIAL SCENE

THE WAR changed many things, including attitudes. The vast majority of Britons had an unreasoned faith in eventual victory, even in the dark days when the nation stood alone in Europe. The necessities of rationing, direction of labour and other controls had produced a leavening hitherto unseen in Britain's class-conscious society. While a public school education gave a good chance of a commission in the services, there were a good few young 'gentry' in the ranks rubbing shoulders with lads from humble homes, just as many a bright boy from a terraced house could be found in an officers' mess. Ex-Roedean girls manned searchlights alongside lasses from the Gorbels; and such mixing was also evident in priority civilian occupations with directed and volunteer labour.

The ingrained 'them' and 'us' attitude brought about by the poverty and unemployment of the 1920s and 1930s was, to a large degree, sublimated through the common cause. At the same time, political awareness spread; the lower income groups did not want to return to 'the old days' when peace arrived. When Russia was attacked and Churchill quickly embraced the Soviets as an ally, the British Communist Party, embarrassed and somewhat discredited by Stalin's duplicity in helping Hitler carve up Poland, now became increasingly active. Although Russia was naïvely presented as a benevolent workers' state, the British working class as a whole tended to be suspicious of Communism. Some of the creed's most faithful adherents were idealists, intellectuals and academics who saw in Marx's work a route to Utopia. The Communist Party had a considerable number of zealots who were active in promoting their propaganda, particularly at worker level in industry, albeit subtly delivered in the cause of victory. The opening of a Second Front, clarion call of the Communists, received willing support from large sections of the community who felt Britain should give the Russians more positive aid. Britain, in no position to mount a cross-Channel invasion, gave immediate support by supplying war equipment. The Royal

▲ The Auxiliary Territorial Service, formed in 1938, included the First Aid Nursing Yeomanry which had a transport branch of which these girls are members. The dispatch-rider's motor cycle has a regulation hooded headlamp which gives a good idea of the meagre amount of light emitted on to the road.

◀ The most famous member of the ATS. HRH Princess Elizabeth.

◀ By mid-war 47 per cent of Balloon Command personnel were WAAFs (Women's Auxiliary Air Force) who also operated more than 1,000 all WAAF balloon sites. Tethering balloons demanded considerable physical stamina, particularly in windy weather. Every open space in London seemed to have its balloon site. This partly deflated silver monster occupied a former playing-field.

▲ WAAFs replaced many men on aircraft maintenance. ACW Doris Bearman, 20 years old, refuels an Anson aircraft.

◀ Back to school; WAAFs did much of the delicate instrument repair. To become proficient there were long hours of technical instruction. The women's services demanded short hair styles but evidently some girls got away with on-the-collar locks, a civilian fashion of the time.

▲ Bedtime reading 1942. A WAAF swots up on the technicalities of aeroplanes. Lacking official textbooks, a pre-war weekly publication provided information.

◄ Like the other services, the Royal Navy used requisitioned mansions for many of its shore establishments. HMS Eaglet at Liverpool was a WRNS (Women's Royal Naval Service) training establishment. Here four young recruits arrive at the reception centre on a bleak winter's day in 1941.

▲ Many women who were qualified pilots served with the Air Transport Auxiliary, delivering all types of aircraft. Here First Officer Joan Naylor prepares to fly a Spitfire from the factory airfield.

◄ The Wrens (WRNS) was considered the more desirable of the women's services if you wanted to be with a 'better class of gal'. In practice things were slightly different. Many of the tasks Wrens undertook were far from ladylike. Here a girl arc welds a reinforcing strip to a landing craft door.

▲ Some five million women went into war industry and tackled a variety of tasks, often dirty and strenuous. Skills had to be learned and a special training school was set up at Slough to teach machine-shop work. Here Miss Ruby May works in a machine-shop.

Navy escorted a number of convoys to north Russian ports at great cost in ships and the lives of merchant seamen. Sailors might survive shells, torpedoes, bombs and bullets, but there was little chance of being rescued alive from the icy sea on that run.

When, in December 1941, Japan attacked Pearl Harbor and the United States entered hostilities, British faith in ultimate victory was reinforced with substance, but during the early months of 1942 general morale was probably at its nadir. The successes in North Africa against Mussolini's forces, which brought the cocky but catchy ballad 'Where Do We Go From Here?' blaring out from radio dance-bands, had given way to retreats when General Rommel and the Africa Corps arrived on the scene.

Inferior and inadequate equipment had again failed the bravery of the British Tommy who, with grudging respect for the enemy, adopted their favourite ballad 'Lilli Marlene' to make it his own. The seemingly pathetic response of British defences to the Japanese invasion of Malaya, the loss of two capital

▲ With a husband in the Army, Mrs Elizabeth Henderson of Gateshead 'did her bit' working on ordnance.

▶ 'When I'm making shells I often say to myself, "That's another one for my son in the Navy."' Mrs Elizabeth Booker, mother of five, chasing and plugging shells in a Sheffield ordnance factory.

◄Women were even to be found in the muscle demanding shipyards of the north. Britain was still building more ships than any other nation at the start of hostilities.

◄For those women whose work was near their homes many local authorities set up nurseries. In the summer of 1942 Flint Green Road Nursery in Birmingham had 22 resident toddlers and children under five whose mothers did night work, plus 20 daily boarders. Here war worker Mrs Rose Sullivan waits after her day shift while a nurse tucks 18-month-old John in the pram beside 3½-year-old sister Maureen.

ships and the ignominious surrender at Singapore darkened the mood at home; it seemed our land and sea forces were stuck with a losing streak. Not until victory in the Battle of El Alamein in the autumn of 1942 did the scene brighten.

Another aspect of the social scene in wartime Britain can be viewed as either a decline in moral standards or a trend towards sexual enlightenment. There was an upsurge in the number of illegitimate births and notified cases of VD increased by well over 100 per cent on pre-war figures. VD had previously been a subject indelicate to mention outside medical circles, but the wartime increase caused the Ministry of Health such concern that a national publicity campaign was launched to highlight the dangers. War and the uncertainty of life for the combatants had always brought increased demand for the services of prostitutes and the Second World War was no exception. But now there was a new aspect of promiscuity. Large numbers of young women in the services or engaged on war work, were enjoying a personal emancipation, very different from their pre-war home environment. While the majority of girls still saved themselves for marriage, the sexual enlightenment of the times weakened the status of chastity. The Second World War accelerated the trend towards what some women saw as liberation and others as equality, even if the majority still happily accepted woman's traditional lot.

Change in the workplace was affected by the one and a half million women who had taken on jobs formerly held by men. Payment could be at rates half or even a third of those of male employees, but during the war, in an increasing number of situations, women won equal pay for equal work. Employers traditionally expected to pay women less and as far as possible resisted this equality, helped by the fact that women were less inclined to join unions. Shortage of manpower both in the armed forces and war industry led, in December 1941, to the introduction of conscription of women. Initially involving those aged 20 to 30 years, there was the option of the women's services or important war work such as the Women's Land Army, armament factories, nursing, civil defence and other specified employment. Initially less than a third opted for the women's services. Eventually, all eligible women between 18 and 51 years were subject to some form of conscription or direction. Britain was the first nation in the Second World War to subject women to conscription.

As austerity took a tighter grip on the Home Front, war production got into its stride. More than 250 new factories were built by the government and thousands of small businesses went over to war work. Component assembly was also undertaken by many of the civil defence organizations that had to sit and wait. The Women's Voluntary Service and other enterprising agencies did similar work, often carried out at home. At the peak, in 1944, more than five million people were engaged in war work plus nearly another million helping part-time in various essential activities. At the time, four and a half million Britons were in military service.

▶ Many women who volunteered for war work had to live in hostels or lodgings near the factories. Mrs Vera Elliott, whose husband was serving overseas with the Argyll and Sutherland Highlanders, was one. Here she is at Sunderland station saying goodbye to her 3-year-old daughter, Heather, who was to be looked after by grandparents.

▶ Far right: The war brought contacts that would have been unlikely to have occurred in peacetime. Once caught up in the London high society whirl, 20-year-old Rachel Bingham worked on a WVS refreshment van in the East End during the Blitz. Here she hands tea to a labourer engaged in clearing a bombsite.

◄In what the Ministry of Labour termed Group 2 employment, women replaced men in many of the service industries. The younger male bus conductors were replaced by conductresses who became known as 'clippies'. Rita Anderson, a serviceman's wife, was a 'clippie' on London buses. (Note the blackout shades round the light bulbs).

►In the cities women took over many of the manual jobs for local authorities. Mrs G. Warren, aged 35, worked as a street cleaner for St Pancras Borough Council, 7a.m. to 4.45p.m. with three meal breaks. Before the war she worked as an office cleaner.

◄The railways had hitherto been largely a male domain. Mrs Cook, with a husband in the Middle East, joined the Great Western Railway and worked the Molland signal box on the Barnstaple line.

►Assembling turrets for Crusader tanks.

In engineering works which had been purely a male domain pre-war, the influx of women on to the shop floor was often not without its problems. At a midlands factory the middle-aged foreman of a machine shop eventually had an all-female shift of operators. He was disconcerted by this development and, being a man of rather narrow views, looked on women as being inferior. He started to treat his women workers in a hectoring manner. Failing to get any acknowledgement of his superiority through this tactic, he then began to address them in terms which would currently be considered as sexual harassment. The women put up with this for a few weeks and then planned to teach him a lesson. At the end of their shift they cornered him in his 'office', held him down and proceeded to apply a large quantity of machine grease to a part of his anatomy. The experience was humiliating enough for the man to ask the management for transfer to another shop. Although he escaped the women it was some weeks before he was rid of the bright purple dye they mixed with the grease.

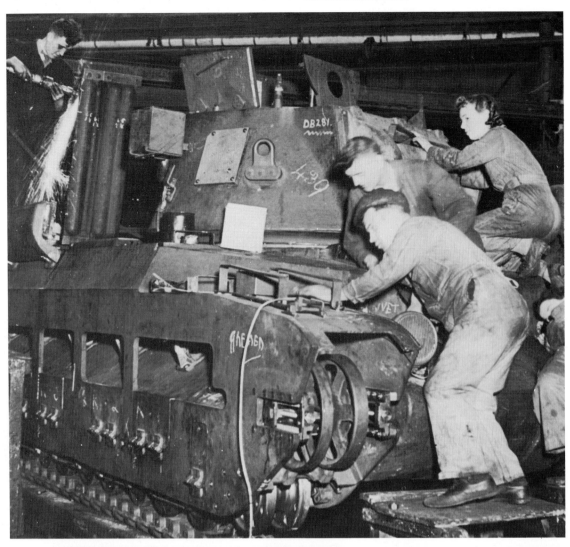

◄ Men and women working on the assembly of a Matilda infantry tank at a northern factory. It took 2,000 man hours to assemble this model.

▼ Below left: Bertie Beale tries a template to a shell casing he has been machining. He had been employed making shells at a Royal Ordnance Factory for 42 years when this photograph was taken in 1941.

▼ Furniture manufacturers were directed to make war equipment fashioned in wood. Here 64-year-old Frank Turner uses a spokeshave to trim the laminated 2-blade training aircraft propellers.

▲Final production line of 4-engined Halifax bombers at Handley Page's Radlett factory. The aircraft industry became a major priority and from 1942 was producing more than 25,000 aircraft a year. The London Passenger Transport Board were among the builders of Halifax bombers.

▶Several furniture firms made parts for the all-wood De Havilland Mosquito. Fuselages of the so-called 'Wooden Wonder' seen prior to assembly at Hatfield, Hertfordshire.

◄ An alternative to military service was the coal mines, a reserved industry which badly needed labour to replace miners who had joined the armed forces. Many conscientious objectors went to the mines, but as a critical shortage arose, in the summer of 1943 one in ten of male conscripts were directed to work in the pits, selection by ballot. It was, to say the least, unpopular and in the estimate of most true miners the newcomers were often more of a liability than an asset. Here two 'Bevin Boys', the popular name for the young mining conscripts and volunteers, exchange a joke with two old hands in Ollerton colliery yard.

◄ To avoid damage by air attack a number of underground factories were set up, the most notable being in old stone quarry workings near Bath. Here there were three million square feet of floor area being utilized to produce aircraft engines. The machine shop, with noise and dust, was not the most pleasant of environments.

► With Russia in the war the British Communist Party whose organ *The Daily Worker* had been banned on 21 January 1941, later blossomed out with posters which were only surpassed in quantity by those from the various 'Ministries'. The demands of this bill evidently amused these Tommies.

▶The WVS turned its hand to many things. Adding the green, brown and black sacking strips to twine in netting to make the camouflage drapings was a regular occupation for one London group. Mrs Waters (left) and Mrs James are at this work in an old school at Addison Road.

▶Far right: In the mid-war years when there was only limited enemy air activity, several Civil Defence organizations with time on their hands took up component assembly work for factories. At this London East End fire station the firemen made up control units for night-fighter radios. To ensure accuracy, the parent factory sent Miss René Milner out each week to inspect and supervise.

THE RED ARMY's Fight is YOUR Fight!

The Communist Party says **ACT NOW!**

★ Remove Pro-fascists from high places
★ End Employers' Mismanagement and Waste
★ Restore T.U. Rights and "Daily Worker"

AID SOVIET–SMASH HITLER

▲ Harry Pollitt, the British Communist Party secretary, with entourage of suitably clad workers, addressing a crowd in Westminster. There were many converts to the Marxist creed during the war, but the 'working class' majority were suspicious of the promised workers' state.

◄ Of far more appeal to the British citizen was the commissioned report of the distinguished academic, Sir William Beveridge. He became a household name following the publication of his social security plan, seen by many as the foundation-stone of the post-war welfare state.

When war production got into full stride there were an increasing number of cases of 'surplus to requirements'. Bureaucracy was embarrassed and looked for ways to reduce the stockpiles. As a result weapons and items of equipment were sometimes issued to people who had received no instruction in using them.

Young Lennox MacLean was ploughing with horses in a cliffside field on the Aberdeenshire coast when Willy, the local coastguard, approached. Lennox asked the man about the peculiar piece of black ironmongery in his hand. He was told, with pride, that it was a Sten gun with which Willy could deal with any Germans he might encounter. Asked how it worked, Willy proceeded to pull and push a lever on the weapon to impress the boy. With a sudden click the whole thing came to pieces and bits fell to the ground. Willy was still trying to reassemble the gun half an hour later as Lennox left the field. The boy could not help commenting that it was a good job the Germans hadn't arrived.

▲ Wartime farewells at Euston Station.

◄ The moment wives or parents lived in fear of. A Post Office messenger boy delivers the orange covered telegram that reports a casualty or missing man.

▼ Below left: Welcome home; Mrs Challoner greets her 18-year-old son John on leave from the Army. Men who were stationed near their homes could take advantage of an occasional 'forty-eight' and spend a night in their own bed. Those farther away had to wait for their week's leave, every three months (in theory). For men sent overseas it was years, not months.

▼ A young mother with a month-old baby in her cottage home at Haddenham, Bucks, summer 1943. Not the happy scene it appears, for Mrs Lydia Comyn had been recently widowed and daughter Annette would never see her father – a soldier who had been killed in action.

ENTERTAINMENT FOR THE PEOPLE

THE IMPORTANCE of radio and cinema in promoting public morale was recognized and fostered from the earliest days of these twentieth-century innovations. The tone of BBC news and newsreel commentaries was decidedly patriotic and often bellicose in this cause. Films with a current war theme invariably conveyed the stiff upper lip image. *The First of the Few*, the story of R. J. Mitchell, the Spitfire designer, played by Leslie Howard, Britain's number one heart-throb of the time; and Noël Coward's naval saga, *In Which We Serve*, loosely based on Louis Mountbatten's destroyer command, both won wide acclaim. There was also a stream of officially sponsored documentaries: *Target for Tonight* (RAF bombers), *Coastal Command* (the air war at sea), *Desert Victory* (the Middle East campaign), *Fires Were Started* (the London Blitz), and a score of others drew long queues at the cinemas.

However, the escapism provided by Hollywood productions still proved the most popular attraction at the 'flicks'. The great names like Clarke Gable, Humphrey Bogart, James Cagney, Edward G. Robinson and the rest attracted packed houses. Hollywood's attempt to portray wartime Britain were less acceptable in that they were usually so far removed from realism as to be irritating to British audiences. Those starring the dashing Errol Flynn, who seemed to specialize in portraying characters who bested the enemy almost single-handed, came in for particular criticism by the Press.

Although cinemas were plentiful and often to be found in the smallest country towns, not everyone had the transportation, opportunity or desire to go to 'the pictures'. Recognizing this, the Ministry of Information sent special projection vehicles with external screens around to venues as varied as sports fields, village greens and town car parks to show a variety of short documentaries, more to inform and condition than entertain.

Apart from news, it was 'the wireless' on which the majority of the population relied for

entertainment, the war years being the heyday of the radio comedian and the catchphrase. 'Hello playmates!' was the opening quip of Arthur Askey in 'Band Wagon', a salutation taken up by the man in the street. 'Band Wagon' was a popular programme at the outbreak of war and built its humour around an absurd plot. In similar vein was 'ITMA – It's That Man Again' featuring Tommy Handley. 'ITMA' eventually became something of a comedy institution with a plethora of catchphrases from characters provided by such talented impressionists as Jack Train and Dorothy Summers. Colonel Chinstrap's 'I don't mind if I do', Mrs Mop's 'Can I do you now Sir?', Ali Oop's 'I go, I come back!', the Diver's 'I'm going down now Sir', were some of the most famous that could be heard up and down the land in all sorts of company when the occasion fitted. There were other popular comedy tune-ins with catchphrases, notably the American flavoured 'Hi Gang!' with Vic Oliver, Ben and Bebe Daniels. Among the stand-up comedians Rob Wilton with his repetitive opening line 'The day war broke out', Cyril Fletcher, the master of the naughty Odd Ode, and Elsie and Doris Waters who, as the

▲ Denham Studios were used for making many of the wartime films. Richard Greene (left) and Valerie Hobson starred in *The Unpublished Story*, a Two Cities production about heroism in the Blitz. Several of the extras playing firemen were members of the Uxbridge Fire Brigade.

► Women in the canteen of a Royal Ordnance factory enjoy one of the twice-a-week ENSA (Entertainments National Service Association) concerts during their lunch break. ENSA was formed in 1939 to entertain servicemen and was extended to industries from mid-1940.

cockney Gert and Daisy, drew laughter from the topical Home Front scene.

Most of this comedy was to be heard on the Forces Programme, brought into operation early in 1940 and, as its name implies, intended primarily to cater for the tastes of those in the services. Because of the generally lighter nature of its programmes it became preferred listening to the BBC's other broadcast, the Home Service, in many civilian households. Popular music occupied much of the Forces time, with regular hour-long contributions from various dance bands. Sentimental ballads were in vogue and the renderings from Vera Lynn undoubtedly the most acceptable. Miss Lynn was acclaimed the 'Forces' Sweetheart' and for many men came to represent an audible link with their women at home. Many of the vocalists heard were American, via the gramophone record, and the most popular voice was that of crooner Bing Crosby.

'Music While You Work' came mid-morning to millions in the factories, relayed on firms' speaker systems that became necessary for air

> *The war disrupted most professional sport although there was no lack of interest or effort in promoting events, albeit the players were locally recruited and often amateurs. At that holy-of-holies for the cricket worshippers, Lord's, the administration made a determined effort to continue staging matches during all the wartime summers, and this despite the presence of the RAF who had requisitioned part of the site. The practice ground was used for drill and the pavilion as a reception centre. One RAF recruit, Albert Herbert, an enthusiast for the game, was amazed to find himself in the hallowed Long Room; 'My intake walked up and down after having "filled a bottle" and taken the "cough test", all with our pants down. I did not dare to think what W. G. Grace would have said about it! Meanwhile, Alf Gover was getting ready to bowl to Wally Hammond. With our trousers back up there was the opportunity to witness a first class game before being marched off to our billet at Viceroy Court. What an experience to relate in later years to all those avid cricket fans to whom Lord's was their Mecca.'*

raid instructions. The BBC Home Service did not neglect classical music or that which some thought of as highbrow. Chamber music was seen as an obvious euphemism by its military detractors. Of general interest and educational programmes a question and answer panel of 1941, becoming 'The Brains Trust' in 1942

attracted a wide and regular audience of listeners. Such was the Brains Trust popularity that the idea was imitated up and down the country in both civilian venues and military camps for popular educational entertainment. Part of this radio programme's attraction was the presence of the two regular members of the team, the intellectual 'Professor' C. E. M. Joad and the anecdotal Commander A. B. Campbell, whose eloquence made them celebrities.

Entertainment was taken to service installations and war production plants by many stage, screen and radio personalities, arranged by ENSA (Entertainments National Service Association). In the factories the most popular comedian was the 'Cheeky Chappie', Max Miller. At a time when sexual matters were still taboo as a subject in public entertainment and the mildest innuendo considered daring, Max Miller had a reputation for going farther in this direction than anyone else. Rumour attributed Max as the originator of many blue jokes but in truth his tales were decidedly mild by 1990 standards. Another extremely popular entertainer whose lyrics were often naughty was the homely George Formby, master of the ukulele. George became famous chiefly through his comedy films, where he played the good-natured blunderer who always triumphed in the end. To many he seemed almost a caricature of Britain in this war.

For those with more elevated tastes, serious music was not neglected and appeared to enjoy a wider audience than pre-war, through the good offices of CEMA (Council for the Encouragement of Music and the Arts) which put on 4,449 concerts in 1943 alone. Surprisingly, a symphony concert orchestra would often draw a full house at the same district venue that had previously been packed to hear Max Miller. The most notable promoter of classical music was the concert pianist Dame Myra Hess who, for much of the war, organized regular lunchtime concerts at the National Gallery – its normal treasures having been secreted in Welsh caves to escape the bombs.

While the Blitz emptied some stages in London's West End, the Windmill Theatre, boasted 'We never closed' for many years thereafter. The Windmill, just off Piccadilly, provided a vaudeville show where many

comedians who rose to fame in post-war years – notably Jimmy Edwards – began their careers. But the Windmill was really famous for its nude showgirls, something then considered exceedingly daring. The law required that unclothed young ladies remain completely stationary while exposed to public gaze on stage – a challenge to a few of the ungallant among the hordes of servicemen attracted to the Windmill. Despite pearl barley peashooters and elastic bands it was another claim of the Windmill showgirls that 'we never moved'.

Never before had there been such a wholesale destruction of books, or such demand for new volumes. Five million volumes were destroyed in the December 1940 fire raids on London. The publishers Blackwoods, Collins, Eyre & Spottiswoode, Hutchinsons, Longmans, Samson Low and Ward Lock had their premises and stocks destroyed. Then there were the continual collection of books and magazines for paper salvage. But books were also collected for the Services, hospitals and hostels. New publications to war economy standard were avidly sought. As evidence of the demand, when HMSO produced a booklet on the Battle of Britain, the initial print of 300,000 soon sold out. Despite paper shortages, 6,747 titles were published in the last year of war, about half that published in 1939.

Magazines flourished and vied with one another for paper allocation. New magazines came out to cater for the Home Guard and Air Training Corps and technical magazines for the war industries were encouraged. A firm favourite of the Forces was the monthly *Lilliput* and many households took *Picture Post* or *Illustrated Weekly* for a pictorial treatment of the world at war.

▲'Workers' Playtime' was a thrice-weekly BBC lunchtime programme staged in factory canteens and other suitable venues for live broadcasting. The audience being entertained by comedians Harry Bennett and Harry Williams appear too well-groomed to have come from the factory floor. The pianists are Ivor Dennis and George Myddleton.

▶In the summer of 1942, RAF Bomber Command began to mount its offensive against German cities. These raids were good morale raisers on the Home Front. The uniformed man buying a paper in St Giles' Circus is a Home Guard officer; no regular army officer would smoke his pipe while walking in the street.

▶During the Blitz the Germans introduced a new weapon specifically to obtain the maximum blast effect. A sea mine was released to float down by parachute, the 1,000kg missile having a particularly devastating effect among buildings. One of these 'land mines' – as the public called them – landed in Latham Street, Poplar on the night of 27/28 July 1941. Taken the following day, the photograph shows one of the casualties being removed from a flattened house. A nearby brick street shelter did not withstand the blast from the explosion.

AND BOMBS STILL FELL

WHEN, in June 1941, Hitler sent his forces east against the Soviet Union, including some 80 per cent of the Luftwaffe that had been busy attacking Britain, the Home Front experienced a respite with limited or no enemy air activity for the rest of that year. But the German bombers that remained in the Low Countries and France continued to torment, particularly with hit-and-run attacks on south and east coast towns and ports. In this respect one of the most troubled towns during six years of war was Great Yarmouth in Norfolk, a seaside holiday town, which received nearly 100 visits from the Luftwaffe.

Not until the spring of the following year were there again any really heavy bombings of our towns and cities, and these came as a direct reprisal against an RAF night attack. On the night of Palm Sunday, 28/29 March 1942, some 250 Bomber Command aircraft ignited the Baltic port of Lübeck in what was, up to that time, the most concentrated bombing of

any German town by the RAF. It produced the highest German civilian casualties so far – more than 300 killed and nearly 800 injured – with an estimate of more than half the houses in the town destroyed or suffering some form of damage. Much of the destruction involved old buildings of historical, religious or architectural value. At Hitler's behest, the Luftwaffe in the west marshalled all available bombers for a series of revenge attacks which became known in Britain as the Baedeker raids. Targets were cities and towns which, like Lübeck, contained buildings of architectural splendour, but whereas the RAF raid had been an 'area attack' designed to immobilize an important port, the German revenge attacks were deliberately aimed at historic and religious centres.

Exeter, Bath, Norwich, York and Canterbury were in turn the objectives during a two-month period; the names suggesting that the Luftwaffe was using the renowned Baedeker Guide as a source for target selection. While no more than 80 bombers were involved in any one attack, the advances in target location and more effective ordnance brought heavy damage and loss of life. As most of these towns and cities had not been considered likely targets, their defences were poor and in the early attacks the RAF night fighter force was caught off guard. The Luftwaffe's campaign began on the night of 24 April with a raid on Exeter and was concluded with a raid on Norwich (which had suffered three previous bombings) on 26/27 June. In a dozen raids on these six locations some 2,500 people were killed. Thereafter enemy activity again subsided to what were generally referred to as nuisance raids. The capital was not an infrequent recipient of this attention which could still result in gruesome casualties. On 23 January 1943 'sneak' raiders, Focke-Wulf Fw 190 fighter-bombers each carrying a 1,100lb bomb, dropped one on Sandhurst Road School, Catford, killing 38 children and six adults and leaving 67 others, mainly children injured.

▶Top right: Lansdown Place, Bath after the 'Baedeker' raids on two successive nights in late April 1942.

▶ During the attacks on Exeter one bomb fell on the south choir aisle of the cathedral.

▲The Guildhall at York blazes during the 28 29 April 1942 bombing.

▲Above right: Canterbury Cathedral towers above some of the ruins resulting from three nights of Luftwaffe attack in June 1942.

►Anderson shelters withstood the worst when these Norwich houses were levelled during a 'Baedeker' raid.

▲Above left: During the 9 May 1942 raid on Norwich, one Dornier Do 217 hit a balloon cable and was brought down in a field at Stoke Holy Cross a few miles from its target. The crew perished.

▲ An addition to the anti-aircraft defences by 1942 was the 'Z' Battery, of twin projectors for 3-inch rockets. Many 'Z' Batteries were manned by Home Guards.

◄The indoor Type T shelter, known as the Morrison, built of steel plate and angle, could also serve as bed and table.

◄To aid firefighters, static water tanks holding 4,000–5,000 gallons, were placed in many streets. This in Bedford Square, London was, like most road obstacles, decked with white paint. The tank also had barbed wire round the edge to deter pranksters and unauthorized use of the water.

LEND A HAND – ON THE LAND

AGRICULTURE had been severely depressed in the twenties and thirties with farmers being unable to compete with the cheap temperate food from abroad. Only in fresh milk and other perishable products, which the foreigner could not supply, was there a modest living to be made. The early fears about Hitler's intentions stirred memories of the U-boat blockade of the Great War and the shortages that had incurred. In the aftermath of the Munich crisis there was serious governmental interest in revitalizing home agriculture. Among the steps taken was the formation of the Women's Land Army (WLA) to provide the extra muscle in a labour intensive industry.

Concern about food supplies was not misplaced for the attrition suffered by our shipping during the early months of hostilities made starvation a possibility, if not a probability. Much farm land, fruitful in the 1914–18 conflict, had since stood neglected. Agricultural output was not something that could be increased in a few months. Implements abandoned by bankrupts had to be retrieved from the nettles and farmers exhorted to speed the plough. And speed it they did, with some six and a half million acres being brought back into cultivation during six years of war. The Ministry of Agriculture, Fisheries and Food devised County War Agricultural Committees to be directors of the rural scene, investing them with considerable powers. Land could be requisitioned and incompetent farmers dismissed. From a farmer's viewpoint the worst aspect of the omnipotent 'War Ag' was its bureaucracy that spawned a persistent deluge of forms and directions.

Pre-war, the approximately 46 million inhabitants of the United Kingdom relied on distant lands for 60 per cent of their food, which came mainly from Canada, Australia, New Zealand, Argentina and the USA. By the end of hostilities the shipments had been reduced by half due to the success of the home-growing campaign. This was achieved despite the loss of 98,000 men to the forces and says much for the 117,000 women who took their places. In 1939 British farming, more or less, picked up where it had left off in 1918 for there had been few developments in the intervening years to alter the pattern of husbandry. Work was still performed largely by hand and horse power. Twenty years of impecuniosity had seen little mechanization and farm tractors were not much more in evidence than in 1919.

The hard work still had to be done by hand as the Land Army girls soon discovered. Many

▼Wartime, down on the farm. A Land Girl drives the dairy herd out into a pasture beside an AA battery where elms help camouflage the gunners' Nissen huts.

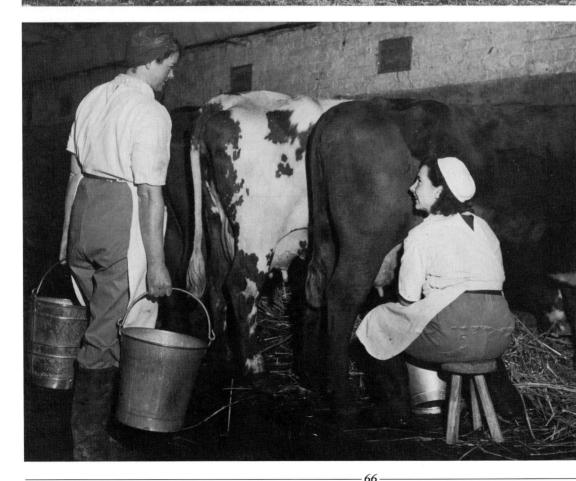

◄ Hardly a craft, but even muck-spreading had to be learned. The WLA had a school farm at Cannington, Somerset, where many new recruits took courses.

►Dorothy Lacey, aged 27, with a barrow full of feed for Rhode Island Reds on a Northamptonshire poultry farm. A former waitress, she was bombed out in both Bristol and Bath before joining the WLA.

◄ The dairy herd at farmer Tupper's Bigno Farm in Sussex was at one time milked by two Land Army girls. Helen Newmarsh, a former shorthand-typist in Worthing, hand milks Cleopatra, while 29-year-old Rosalind Cox carries the milking pails to the dairy. Cowshed work was fatiguing, twice a day, every day.

►Pitching sheaves at harvest time was hard, tiring work but enjoyed by many WLA girls. Joan Day, seen in an oat field on Hallow Moor, Mount Barton, Devon, was a former dressmaker and left for the land in February 1942.

mistakenly believed agriculture was a soft alternative to the women's services, resulting in a fairly high turnover as the disillusioned and physically beaten turned to other work. Many girls with urban backgrounds – one in two recruits – found the dirty, tiring job of pulling and topping sugar beet or pitching wheat sheaves far too demanding on strength. Others took to the life and loved it, particularly if they had to work with animals. While some two-thirds of the girls worked for individual farmers, there were WLA hostels all over the country whence all-girl gangs went out to work on War Ag or Forestry Commission land. About 100,000 women joined the WLA, although its strength was never much more than 80,000 at any one time.

An additional source of labour was through the re-employment of pensioners who had been farm labourers, and in most villages there were those who would 'lend a hand on the land' after their normal daily occupations; postmen, butchers, school masters and the like. A labour force, typical of the late war years, on one 300-acre farm in the eastern counties, consisted of five WLA girls, two boys under 18, one 30-year-old unfit for military service, two men in their fifties and four over 65. Another source of labour were the volunteer parties of German and Italian prisoners of war. It was a fairly universal opinion among farmers that while the former were diligent, the Italians were generally disinclined to do much work. Some 130,000 Italians were active in forestry and agriculture by 1943 and 90,000 German PoWs by the end of the war. Agriculture was also a reserved occupation, a fact that brought a few inexperienced individuals into the industry to masquerade as farmers. But in this respect agriculture was not alone as a haven for those who wanted to evade military service without bearing the stigma of being a conscientious objector.

Additional to the farm effort to provide more home-grown food was the not inconsiderable contribution of allotment holders and home gardeners. Three and a half million allotments were tended, many created in parks, playing fields and village greens. Even roadside verges were cultivated in some areas. Mechanization helped and by 1942, the number of tractors in use had risen to 150,000.

Many young women who forsook urban employment for patriotic duty with the Women's Land Army received a culture shock when exposed to life on the farm. Jane Rhodes had dreams of toil in a pleasant rustic setting. The reality of her first week on a Lancashire holding was the stench and dust of cleaning poultry sheds between the morning and evening barrowing of manure from a cowshed through muck and slush. The last straw was the answer her employer gave her to her inquiry as to where the lavatory was situated: 'Men go behind bramble bushes in't meadow, but if tha's worried about thorns tha can go behind haystack.' Jane gave her notice and joined the ATS and a gentler life.

▲Under a cascade of chaff and oat straw from the 'pitcher', Ben Simpson, aged 19, helps stack the residue from the thrashing machine. This was hot, dirty and itchy work. Ben was one of the seasonal volunteers from towns who spent their holidays working on farms for the flat rate of a shilling an hour. Ben's regular job was in a London radio valve factory; in this summer of 1943, he was staying in a Youth Service Camp at Nunney, Somerset.

◄In the mid-war years 700,000 old-age pensioners had returned to work, many in agriculture. Here 71-year-old Harry King carries his wheat straw yelms up a rick he is thatching at Peyton Hall, Manuden, Essex. Agricultural workers in their seventies were a familiar sight on farms during the early 1940s.

▼Forestry work where all timber had to be sawn by hand was also a demanding occupation. These girls, wearing the standard green sweaters and berets and light brown breeches, cross-cut a trunk in a conifer plantation at Culford, Suffolk.

▶Bombs and bullets hit many farms, but Gilbert Mitchell's near Dover had also to contend with German coastal artillery shells fired from the French coast. Here Mr Mitchell and his ploughman keep a wary eye on the sky above the white cliffs.

▶In the later years of hostilities, German prisoners of war were often to be seen in British fields. This gang are engaged in the back-straining job of pulling and shaking sugar-beet.

▶Potatoes being dug at Kew. The famous gardens grew vegetables, mostly for Ministry of Food experiments and trials. Potatoes as food acquired a new status with Potato Bars being opened, the first in London on 14 February 1941.

IN THE SKY

WHILE there was reclamation of a million acres for farming, much existing agricultural land was lost to the needs of the services and government agencies, some 600,000 acres of the total 800,000 acres acquired. This was equivalent to a county the size of Gloucestershire. By far the largest part went for army battle ranges where in some places whole villages were taken over and the population moved out. But some 300,000 acres, often top quality agricultural land, were taken for the proliferation of airfields that appeared wherever the terrain was suitable. In East Anglia and neighbouring regions, airfields dotted the landscape, often only a few miles apart. These self-contained installations, each comprising barracks, workshops, hangars, electrical generating stations and sewage plants in addition to the flying field, cost more than £1 million each. In fact, the airfield building programme was the largest civil engineering project ever undertaken in the United Kingdom. The airfields also undoubtedly provided the most notable of all wartime blots on the landscape, 444 of them having been built during these years. The largest proportion of airfields were built to sustain the combined Anglo-American air offensive against the German war machine.

For civilians the sight and sound of RAF Bomber Command and the USAF aircraft in the skies above provided the most tangible evidence that the enemy was receiving a dose of the same medicine that he had meted out. From the south and south-eastern coasts of England, RAF fighter formations flew 'sweeps' over occupied France and the Low Countries and light and medium bombers struck at enemy airfields, ports and a variety of military targets within their range, eventually to be joined by the US 9th Air Force. This tactical American air arm had the mission of supporting the cross-Channel invasion, as did the RAF's 2nd Tactical Air Force, both organizations eventually moving to the continent to follow the successful break-out from the Normandy bridgehead. The Hurricanes and Blenheims of the early days gave way to Bostons,

The magic of the name Spitfire in the RAF's magnificent defence, stirred the country to finance more. Spitfire Funds sprang up all over the country arranged by hundreds of organizations; for £5,000 a fighter would be named after a county, town, firm, service or individual. Similarly the sum of £20,000 was set for a bomber. The response from the Commonwealth was even greater with large sums donated to equip squadrons.

Ingenious were some of the methods of collection. Manchester and Stockport sold Spitfire Fund tickets on their public transport. Farmers charged to see wrecks of German aircraft on their land, proceeds to a Spitfire Fund. Not to be outdone, one farmer charged to enter 'The only field in Kent without a crashed German aircraft'.

*Most names were well chosen; the BBC gave 'Ariel', Hoover's named theirs 'Skysweeper', while 'Gingerbread' was the result of the Redheads' Spitfire Fund. Other names took a little working out; 'The Old Lady' was donated by the Bank of England staff of Threadneedle Street, 'Yr Hen Bont' was the name for Pontypridd's Spitfire, but for 'Warden of London' the donor did not wish his name disclosed. The **Nursing Mirror** Fund chose to give Hurricanes, named appropriately 'Nightingale' and 'Night Duty' as both served in the same night-fighter squadron before being sent as aid to Russia – a matter over which donors had no control. While some naïve individuals may have thought that they were increasing the number of aircraft, the money went into the general funding of the war effort. Donors did receive a photograph of an aircraft inscribed with the name of their choice and Air Ministry Public Relations 1940–2 kept a brief record of the aircraft for answering queries from the Press and public. Donations continued throughout the war.*

◄ There always seemed to be someone up above. The all too familiar sight of vapour trails high in the blue. Here a squadron of fighters curves over the clouds. In some conditions the trails formed by the engine exhausts in the freezing air merged to form an overcast.

▶ Back from another 'sweep' in mid-1942, Spitfires coming in to land at Rochford. These particular aircraft were piloted by American volunteers in one of the three so-called Eagle Squadrons.

▲ Bombing-up a giant Stirling bomber at Marham, Norfolk in the spring of 1942. The Stirling, the first of the three Bomber Command four-engine types to enter service, could deliver six tons of bombs at short range. A poor flight ceiling made the aircraft vulnerable to enemy defences.

Mitchells, Mosquitoes and new marks of Spitfire, and soon the inhabitants of Essex, Kent, Sussex and the rest of the southern counties learned to recognize the US Marauders, Havocs, Thunderbolts, Mustangs and Lightnings.

It was from bases farther north that the real slogging match took place with the offensive air war being pursued on a major scale. Strategic bombing, planned to destroy the enemy's munition factories, oil supplies, communications, etc., denying him the equipment and materials essential to his war effort to bring him to a point of surrender. To this end the RAF built up Bomber Command with its Stirlings, Halifaxes and Lancasters deployed mainly in Cambridgeshire, Yorkshire and Lincolnshire, more than a thousand strong at peak. The American 8th Air Force eventually numbered more than 2,000 Liberators and Fortresses. RAF Bomber Command operated by night and the 8th Air Force by day, hauling huge tonnages of high-explosives and incendiaries, in a prolonged and costly campaign which only came close to its goal in the closing stages of the war. Some 57,000 British and

▲The idea of a form of kindergarten for the RAF resulted in Britain's first state-promoted quasi-military youth organization, the Air Training Corps, for boys aged between 16 and 18 years. The ATC soon boasted 200,000 members, organized into squadrons and issued with RAF uniforms. Suitable candidates for flight training were identified before they were eligible for RAF service. Glider piloting was a popular activity with the ATC. Cadet George Metcalfe of 1481 Squadron, West Norwood, was accepted for aircrew training (hence the white cap flash) and was scheduled to join the RAF early in 1944.

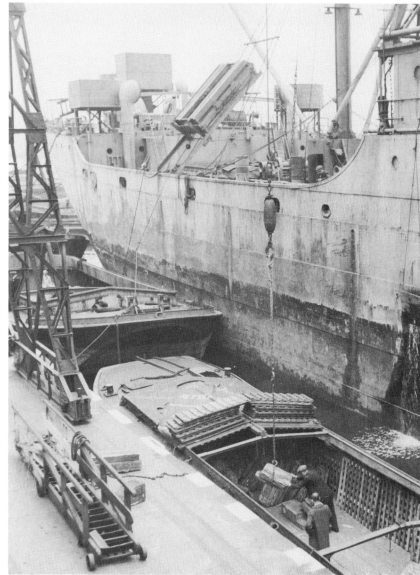

28,000 American airmen were lost in these operations.

For people who lived in the vicinity of Bomber Command airfields sleep was regularly disturbed by the roar of a succession of unseen aircraft climbing away into the night or returning with the occasional dread explosion as some stricken machine did not make safe haven. For people in East Anglia the vast morning assemblies of American bombers and their afternoon homecomings provided an extraordinary spectacle. Often several hundred aircraft could be seen at one time streaking the heavens with vapour trails. In good flying weather the noise of aircraft engines was incessant and the sky seemed always occupied. Air activity over the United Kingdom reached its zenith on 6 June 1944 when the cross-Channel invasion was launched. The Allied air armadas totalling some 10,000 fighters, bombers and transports is still reckoned the greatest assembly of aircraft in one locality in the history of manned flight.

AT SEA

BY THE BEGINNING of 1943 the corner had been turned in the so-called Battle of the Atlantic. U-boats were still sinking merchant ships but at a perilous cost to themselves. The Allied navies and air forces were in the ascendancy and so successful at hunting the enemy submarines that they eventually extracted a toll in casualties among U-boat crews that, as a percentage of total personnel, was far greater than for any other branch of an enemy or Allied service. In the first years of the war at sea shipping was being sunk at a far greater rate than shipyards could produce new vessels. With the United States getting into full production, particularly with the prefabricated and speedily built Liberty ships, there was no longer any major threat to Britain's supplies.

In the late 1930s, if no longer the workshop of the world, Britain remained a major exporter of manufactured goods and possessed the world's largest merchant fleet, some 4,000 registered vessels, to carry these wares and bring the commodities on which the nation depended. Merchant seamen were in the front line from the very first day of the war and could not sail without apprehension until the last. An estimated 30,000 who left British ports during the six years of war never returned. Of those sailors serving with the merchant fleet in 1939, about 75 per cent had been killed or invalided out by 1945. A nation for whom the merchant fleet was then its lifeline probably did not fully appreciate the sacrifice, as during hostilities the scale of losses was hidden in order that the enemy should not know his success in sinkings. The slogan 'We won't waste it sailor' was published as a governmental reminder to the public of the perils the merchant seamen faced on the oceans. This and similar slogans appeared in restaurants and shops, and were even on stickers placed beside the filler caps of new farm tractors.

At the outbreak of war, the Royal Navy was numerically superior to the German fleet even if many of its ships were technically inferior. The U-boat was not only a threat to merchantmen, as the Royal Navy was painfully re-

minded when, a few weeks after war was declared, *U 47* crept into the Scapa Flow anchorage and torpedoed the battleship *Royal Oak*. After Dunkirk, most capital ships were kept chiefly in the Western Approaches and several Scottish sea lochs provided havens as well as assembly locations for Atlantic convoys. There was no guarantee of complete security anywhere in the UK and Luftwaffe bombers from Norway often sought out shipping on the west coast of Scotland. Naval development on the east coast was chiefly defensive, in particular protecting coastal freighters which suffered heavy losses during the early years. Air and sea attacks on such vessels were sometimes in full view of people on the coast, making a particularly demoralizing experience of seeing a merchantman sunk while being unable to do anything to help the victims.

Most ports had some sort of naval presence, particularly minesweepers, to deal with the persistent mining of coastal waters by both the

▲ Charles Piper joins his first ship. A former postman, he was one of many who volunteered for service in the Merchant Navy and underwent three months' training before going to sea. Most volunteers did not realize the high casualty rate in the Merchant Navy.

German navy and air force. At bases around the country, motor- gun- and torpedo-boat flotillas operated against the enemy's coastal shipping and their protectors, the similar E-boats. Also regularly active from many locations were the high-speed Air Sea Rescue launches which retrieved airmen unfortunate enough to come down in the sea. The red-white-and-blue roundels, painted on their hulls, indicated that they were RAF manned. Sea rescues were still performed by the RNLI lifeboats which also faced air attack.

Perhaps the most hazardous undertaking at sea within range of Luftwaffe aircraft was fishing. The fishing fleet had half its vessels requisitioned by the navy during 1939 and 1940 – more than 800 trawlers – of which a third were lost to enemy action, most while serving as improvised minesweepers. Where possible, those that remained to ply their proper trade were provided with machine-gun defence but this proved no deterrent to the heavily armed and armoured Junkers and Dorniers. If well out to sea there was also the risk of being shot up by 'friendly' aircraft who might mistakenly believe that they had come across an enemy-operated vessel. Several fishermen were killed by Allied bullets. In contrast to pre-war days when there were often no buyers for catches, the wartime market could never be satisfied. Fish was never rationed because supplies were too erratic; catches were zoned to save on rail transportation. On the other hand, prices climbed to as much as five times those of peacetime.

◄ Few merchant sailors could match George Lappin's unenviable record. During 27 years at sea four of his ships had been torpedoed and he was the only survivor of one. Despite these experiences and an injured spine, he still wanted to go back to the Merchant Navy.

▼ James Campbell, a 16-year-old cabin boy, on a doomed merchantman in a convoy to Russia, survived with these horrific injuries. He lost his right leg below the knee, half of his left foot and four fingers from his left hand. James spent many months in Scottish hospitals.

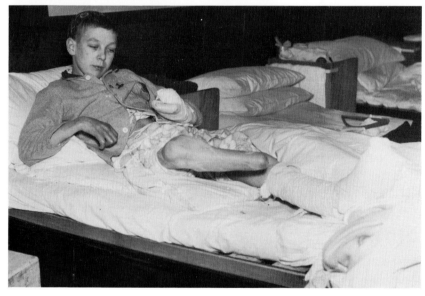

◄ An MTB of the flotilla commanded by Lieutenant-Commander P. G. C. Dickens, great-grandson of Charles Dickens, returns to base at Lowestoft after a patrol.

►A regular presence in Holy Loch from 1941, HMS *Forth* a submarine depot ship, with her brood. The third submarine from the right is a captured German U-boat.

▼WRNS power in a longboat. Such a sight cheered a sailor, if the purpose mystified him. Destroyers *Forester* (far left), *Viceroy* (right) and the armed trawler *Stora* tied up at Grangemouth.

►RNLI crews rescued many sailors and airmen from the sea during the war. The Dungeness lifeboat picked up the pilot of a Messerschmitt Bf 109 (Uffz Bley) on 7 October 1940 and brought him to captivity in Britain.

▲A popular meeting-place for sailors of all services and many nationalities was the Seven Seas Club in Edinburgh. It provided a 'berth' for the mixture of matelots who were 'in port' and far from home. Ludvic Marum (left) and J. Craamer (right) from Norway and the Netherlands respectively, watch players Charles Stalder, Harry Reynolds, Paul Grossman and Olaf Tier (three Americans and a Norwegian).

SAVING AND SALVAGE

THE PATTERN of life in Britain remained little changed during the last two years of hostilities. Austerity held sway with restrictions and shortages a constant feature; many items had disappeared from the shops completely. But rationing, if occasionally adjusted to meet contingencies, was not extended. The Government's controlled economy was firmly established, if sometimes wasteful. People's acceptance of the situation was founded on the common cause of seeking victory. Acceptance was to some extent conditioned by the propaganda of the various Ministries, which never slackened in their exhortations to the public.

Slogans became very much a part of the everyday scene in Britain, particularly in urban areas where advertising hoardings proclaimed advice and encouragement on what to do and what not to do to aid the war effort. The most numerous were those demanding that people save. Money put into savings helped finance the war effort, or so the nation was led to believe. Various savings drives were staged throughout the country, often with a special theme to buy aircraft for the RAF, ships for the navy and the like. The main purpose of the savings campaign was simply to dampen monetary inflation; holding the national purse the government did not have to depend on the people to lend it money to pursue the requirements of war. However, the National Savings movement had vigorous support throughout the community and if social events were organized they were invariably in aid of some savings venture. Savings certificates and savings stamps were the common prizes in any competitive event. Everybody, it was urged, from the very old to the very young could do their bit to help the war effort by saving.

That the majority of households held some savings certificates or were involved in some savings scheme was partly due to the shortages of goods in the shops; in short, there was little of value to buy. Prices of many articles did rise but wartime controls never let inflation get out of hand despite there being more money in circulation. Workers in many industries connected with war production were earning

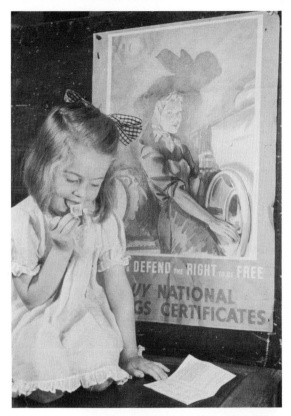

◄ A posed photograph with the object of promoting National Savings. Licking her savings stamp is Heather Scott of Lewknor, Oxfordshire.

► With increases in income tax and lowering of the exemption limit, four million more wage earners became liable for contributions. To sweeten the pill, part of the taxes were to be paid back after the war as Post War Credit. When peace came the government procrastinated on payment and by the time they did pay out, inflation had eroded much of their value.

► Fund raisers at Grove Park, Lewisham during 'Warship Week'.

◄ On a Savings Day at Lewknor village school, Joan Hartwell buys a sixpenny stamp from her teacher. Thirty of these stamps bought a 15s. (75 pence) National Savings Certificate with a promised value of £1.0s.6d. (102½ pence) after ten years.

► As part of the intensive salvage campaign, bales are being delivered to a waste-paper recycling plant.

Certificate of Post-War Credit

1941-42

This is to Certify that the undermentioned sum has been recorded in

favour of .... as the Post-War Credit due

for the year ended 5th April, 1942, under Section 7 of the Finance Act, 1941.

H.M. Inspector of Taxes,

£   :   :

Date.

good wages in comparison with those of the late thirties so that, with an increase in income tax during 1941, an additional four million persons were made liable for assessment. Further tax changes would add another four million before the end of the war. In 1944 the Pay As You Earn scheme was introduced whereby employees' tax was deducted and passed to the tax office by employers, a move resented by the latter, who objected to being the government's unpaid tax collectors.

A further bar to spending was Purchase Tax, introduced in 1941 as a direct tax on purchased goods, with an initial top rate of 33⅓ per cent, but not applicable to food and certain other essentials. Taxes were, inevitably, elevated as the government saw fit and inflation remained more or less in check. A box of matches still cost one penny in 1945, the same as in 1939 – but some boxes had fewer matches. Most desirable luxuries, however, being outside price control, had shown considerable movement. A book retailing at ten shillings in 1939 was 25 shillings in 1945 and with much poorer paper quality.

Another type of saving encouraged throughout hostilities involved material things. People were persuaded to consider if anything they were about to throw away had another use. Could it substitute for something in short supply or provide useful salvage material? Jam jars, bottles, envelopes, wrapping paper and string were among the items to be saved for re-use. Newspapers could find a variety of uses ranging from toilet paper to draught-stopping material. If a use could not be found in your own home, the waste went for salvage. Paper was collected for repulping, leather for fertilizer, bones made glue and explosives or bone meal, and rags could be reclaimed for yarn. Kitchen waste was also collected in towns and processed into the so-called Tottenham Pudding for pig feed.

The collection of various types of salvage was mostly done on a voluntary basis, a task such organizations as the Women's Voluntary Service and Boy Scouts could undertake regularly for the 'cause'. Further, people were asked to part with those household articles which were made of scarce and valuable metals, notably aluminium. The patriotic cast out teapots and saucepans. Promotion of

▲Leather boots by the thousand. The best were reconditioned, the rest made into agricultural fertilizer.

◄ An estimated 50,000 kitchen utensils were turned in in response to Minister of Aircraft Production Lord Beaverbrook's appeal for 'virgin aluminium'. Kettles and pans were put into a smelter, but both process and reclaimed product were too expensive for the salvage to be productive.

▲ Woollen socks – many looking far too good for waste – being sorted for wool reclamation.

salvage drives was accompanied by Ministry of Information propaganda giving the supposed number of aluminium saucepans needed to build a Spitfire and other inspiring information. The donors often became disenchanted when the aluminium pile built with the help of their contribution remained at the local collection point for some months. There was similar displeasure at the loss of cast-iron railings from private and public places which were compulsorily removed. This metal collection also too often languished in the collection heaps. There is a story that a man who had gallantly given his ornamental front gate was so incensed to see it still lying in a scrap merchant's yard 18 months later that he retrieved it. In such circumstances it is understandable that enthusiasm for salvage drives eventually became dampened. However, the collections that lingered did prove an important material reserve if ever urgently required.

If rationing, shortages and patriotism necessitated household savings, frugality was continually cautioned in other respects. People were reminded not to keep a tap running when washing their hands, to use no more than five inches of water in a bath, never to leave an electric light bulb switched on in an empty room, and more. Finally, if one ventured from home, you were cautioned by a glaring official poster, 'Is your journey really necessary?'

► Rubber. Aircraft and vehicle tyres. Those that were sound went for retreading.

▲ Boy Scouts and Sea Scouts collecting newspapers and magazines using an ex-tradesman's horse and cart at Balderton, Nottinghamshire.

▶ Slogans, slogans everywhere. Even Marble Arch served as a hoarding.

◀ Kitchen waste. Cooked up, it produced this foul-smelling pig-feed known as 'Tottenham Pudding' after the original installation. These men are transferring the solidified feed into hessian sacks for transport.

▶ The iron railings are removed for salvage outside the ARP post at 50 Rotherhithe Old Road, Bermondsey, London.

Savings publicity even included school children who were encouraged to buy savings stamps with their pocket money. Special films to promote savings were taken round to schools and shown as part of the campaign. These were popular with pupils if for no other reason than that they made a break from normal lessons. One film featured a ditty sung to the tune of 'Sailor Sailor'. This ran: 'Saving, saving, helping to win the war. Whenever you think you've saved enough, go and save some more.' The compere at a showing of this film at a boys' grammar school suggested that 'Whenever you are bored, boys, just sing this song and everyone else will join in. That's an order.' Of course, this pronouncement was quickly used to advantage by certain of the pupils. The whole Fifth Form burst into patriotic song at the next algebra lesson. After the school had resounded to 'Saving, Saving' on three or four occasions, a stern warning of corporal punishment from the Head restored order. The National Savings people were not invited to that school again.

◄ A need for binoculars by the services brought posters with this message. But Guinness and Famel still offered relief from blues on a damp December day in 1941 near the Grosvenor Hotel, Victoria, London.

► The messages may have been simple but posters were often clever and subtle.

◄ That cough mixture was still in evidence the following winter in Trafalgar Square when Nelson's Column 'did its bit' with a Savings message. As can be seen, the pigeons did not evacuate wartime London.

► Only one of these hoardings in a London street advertises commercial products, the others tell you to walk, dig, save, do war work and go easy on fuel. You would have been fortunate to buy a bottle of whisky, but the distillers still thought it worthwhile to keep up the reminder.

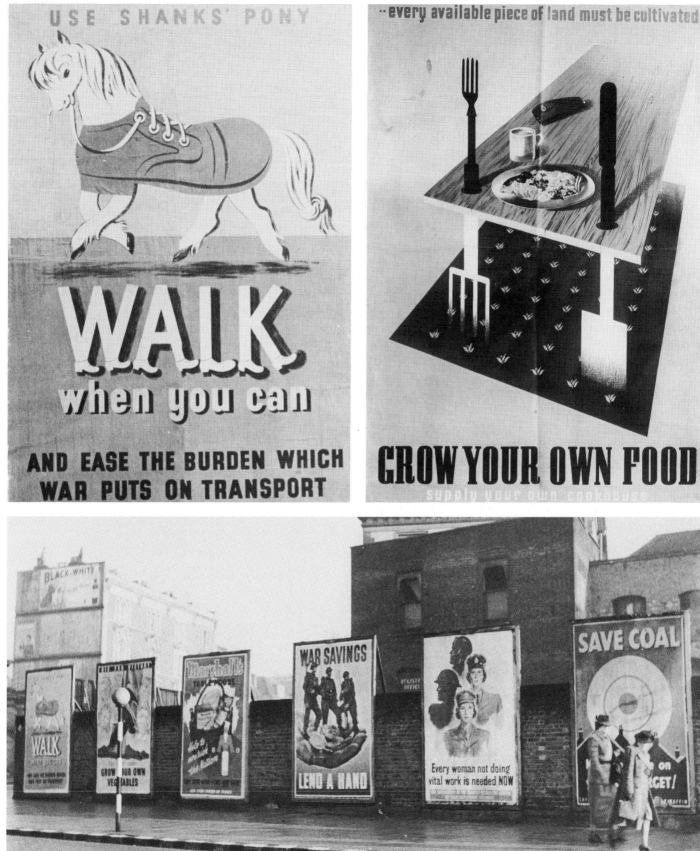

WELCOME STRANGERS

By the middle years of the war, the foreigner in uniform had become commonplace in Britain. In certain areas or in the vicinity of particular army camps or airfields, Poles, Frenchmen or a dozen other nationalities were more in evidence than local men of similar age. There was a strong presence from the Commonwealth brought by the many army and air force units that swelled the numbers of the cosmopolitan assembly in these islands. However, the servicemen who undoubtedly made the greatest impact on wartime Britain were those of the US forces. A million and a quarter of them passed through the UK between early 1942 and the summer of 1945; some were here for but a few weeks or months before participating in the North Africa and Normandy landings, whereas many, assigned to the air forces, were here for three years.

Because GIs, the term for American soldiers derived from GI (for General Issue) stamped on their equipment, were paid three times more than their British counterparts, they were not universally popular with our servicemen. Another cause of resentment was the GIs' access to their base Post Exchanges, stores where they could purchase requisites not easily available to British women, such as nylon stockings and scented soap. The friendly and bountiful GI was a welcome brightness for many girls in the austerity dull days, a not inconsiderable total of 60,000 becoming GI brides. In the greater East Anglian region where the US heavy bomber force was based, American uniforms had become more common than British by the summer of 1944. It was not only the girls who took to the GIs; their mums and dads found canned fruit, chocolate bars, cigarettes and other rare commodities coming their way. And the GI was genuinely motivated in his generosity by a quest for friendship. Many of the associations that were forged by the long stayers were to endure for a lifetime.

▼ Below left: French sailors, with their distinctive hats, buying a copy of *La France Libre*, one of the French language publications produced in the UK after the fall of France. This newspaper shop in Charing Cross Road also catered for Norwegian, Polish and Czech readers.

▼ Foreign nationals serving in the British forces were identified by shoulder titles. The battledress uniform is British, but the cap insignia is of the Norwegian forces.

▲Australian soldiers marching down an English road. The bush hat distinguished the Anzac troops.

►The Empire Rendez-vous Bureau at 18 Northumberland Avenue, London entertained men and women from every part of the British Commonwealth and Empire. During an official visit, the Queen talks to Sergeant Schermer, a South African sculptor, and Aircraftman Pat Mallory, previously a Rhodesian mine manager.

◄ Pilot Officer Pierre Henri Clostermann, who formerly worked for the British News Service in South America, wears a French Air Force uniform at this interview in March 1943. Clostermann later became the most successful French fighter pilot flying for the RAF.

◄ By 1944 'GIs on Pass' crowded into Central London. This was Leicester Square on a winter's day.

▼ 'Now how does this money go?' A Piccadilly rose seller has a customer with the badge and bars for marksmanship and gunnery expertise.

The prospect of forced separations quickened the pace of courtships and the war years saw an upsurge in marriages. Many British girls fell for foreign servicemen, particularly continental charmers, so exciting compared with the reserved conduct of their own country's men. A showgirl from London's Windmill Theatre fell in love with a handsome French captain and married him. He was absent for several weeks at a time. All she knew was that he was engaged in very secret and highly dangerous duties, but guessed – correctly – that he visited France as a contact with resistance groups. Eventually he did not return and she feared the worst. A child had been born and the girl faced up to young widowhood like so many other girls at that time. After hostilities it came as a shock to discover that the handsome charmer had returned to a wife and family in France whom he had apparently been visiting during his clandestine visits. The philosophy that all is fair in love and war was all too prevalent between 1939 and 1945.

▲ Probably the only Londoners in sight are the pigeons. Trafalgar Square with Belgian officers and NCOs in the foreground; Canadians, Americans, Yugoslavs and the ubiquitous Scots in the background.

▶ Preparations for D-Day. Row upon row of British and American army vehicles in a Midlands park, May 1944.

DOODLEBUGS AND ROCKETS

WITH THE REDUCTION in Luftwaffe activity over Britain after the spring of 1941 there had been a gradual return of many evacuees to their homes in the towns and cities. The small force of enemy bombers remaining in France and the Low Countries continued periodic harassing raids, but in 1943 their attentions were turned chiefly to attacking airfields in eastern England whence the ever-growing Anglo-American bomber force launched its missions to Germany. When RAF Bomber Command kept up a sustained bombing of Berlin in the winter of that year, Hitler was moved to order retaliatory raids on London. Those in the metropolis who thought the Blitz was confined to history were persuaded otherwise on the night of 21/22 January 1944 when more than 100 German bombers arrived to deposit some 250 tons of high-explosive and incendiary bombs. Nor was this to be a lone occasion, for in the course of the next twelve weeks another thirteen raids were made, taking the lives of more than 900 Londoners.

During the same period the Luftwaffe increased its activity against airfields in East Anglia and struck at west coast ports which the Germans assumed were handling the ever-growing cargoes from American arsenals. Nor was poor old Hull, a favourite Luftwaffe port target on the east coast, forgotten during this period. But trespass on British airspace during darkness was no longer like the easy forays of 1940. With the aid of improved airborne radar the night sky became a much more dangerous place and despite Luftwaffe concentration of attack and countermeasures, the 'Baby Blitz' of 1944 cost it some 30 bombers.

Comparative quiet settled again and with the cross-Channel invasion of 6 June 1944 it seemed the Luftwaffe would be too busy to stage further assaults on British cities. Unbeknown to the man in the street, Hitler's long-boasted reprisal weapon for the bombing of Germany was about to make its début. Allied intelligence agencies had known of the existence of these weapons for some time and during the winter of 1943/4 had directed a considerable tonnage of bombs against struc-

▲ Firemen set up hoses to quench the fire in shops smashed by a V-1 on 17 June 1944. Clapham Junction's *The Surrey Hounds* had 'had it' too.

This photograph was taken three minutes after the missile struck.

▼ A constable consoles an old gentleman who sits in the rubble of his home in South London while Civil Defence workers retrieve his worldly goods.

► From a Fleet Street rooftop the photographer caught a V-1 in its plunge to earth after the engine stopped.

▼ A column of smoke and debris rises from the Aldwych area where a V-1 struck, seen from crowded Fleet Street – there was often little time to seek shelter because the doodlebugs came at any time of the night and day, and the air raid alert was continuous.

tures in French coastal areas that were connected with this threat. Hopes that the threat would diminish with the D-Day landings was short-lived. In the early morning darkness of 13 June 1944 the first *Vergeltungswaffe Einz* (Reprisal Weapon 1) was launched against Britain – the target central London.

Basically the V-1 was a flying-bomb, and this became the offical descriptive term. More accurately it was a small, expendable aircraft carrying a 1-ton warhead. The power, provided by a simple ram-jet engine speeding the missile at almost 400 miles per hour, gave it an unmistakable audio calling-card, described as akin to an unsilenced, rough-running motor cycle. Soon V-1s were being launched at London at the rate of 100 every 24 hours with perhaps three-quarters avoiding the defences ranged against them. A reorganization of the defences into zones involved barrage balloons and anti-aircraft guns moving south from the capital. Together with improved tactics by fighters that were fast enough to catch them, it was reckoned by mid-July that two-thirds of V-1s launched were being shot down.

Although the firings from the Pas-de-Calais area tailed off during July they did not cease until Montgomery's forces overran the area in August during the advance towards Antwerp. However, by this date V-1s were being air-launched from Heinkel He 111 bombers, some at London, others at the invasion port of Southampton. During the bombardment about 2,340 V-1 flying-bombs reached the general London area and killed 5,745 people while injuring 16,000. The 'doodlebugs' or 'buzz

> *Tractor driver Leslie Parker's thatched cottage crested a hill between the Black Brook and the River Stour on the Essex-Suffolk border. In the early morning of 5 September 1944 he was awakened by the unmistakable noise of a V-1 flying-bomb. Jumping from bed he looked out of the south-facing window, expecting to see the missile's flaming tail. During the summer months the odd V-1 had overflown London and come this way but now, although the noise was growing louder by the second, he still could not see the approaching instrument of destruction. Then, to his horror, the flaming, pulsating monster suddenly appeared in front of him, directly level with his bedroom window, speeding up the valley east to west and not south to north as anticipated. It was probably no more than 50 feet away from the cottage as it passed. Moments later the bomb impacted and exploded on the edge of the A12 road a mile away. The cottage survived with a modest shaking. This was the first occasion that V-1s had been launched from aircraft over the North Sea, this particular missile proceeding at little more than 100 feet up the Stour estuary and river valley until it encountered rising ground.*

bombs' as they were popularly called, exploded before penetration, thus causing the maximum blast damage. It was estimated that the V-1 destroyed or damaged, in varying degrees, a million properties in London and its suburbs.

The weapon brought a third exodus from London; the evacuees went back to their old rural haunts again without waiting for officially organized movement, although this did occur. With the taking of the launching sites in the Pas-de-Calais many thought it safe to return and could not understand why the government still warned against this through the news media. The reason was Reprisal Weapon No. 2 which, for many Londoners, became the most testing of all the types of ordnance aimed at them by the Germans. V-2 was a missile powered by a rocket motor that could lift its twelve and a half tons, including a 1-ton warhead, 60 miles into the stratosphere from the launching sites in eastern Holland to descend at 3,600 miles per hour on London 200 miles away. The first arrived on 8 September 1944 at Chiswick and another 517 hit the London area before the last firing on 27 March 1945. This masterpiece of German wartime technology nevertheless had only a 37 per cent success rate as under half the V-2s fired landed outside the intended target area, the remainder either falling into the sea or exploding in the air.

In an effort to deny the enemy information as to where the missiles fell, early strikes were passed off as exploding gas mains. There was

▲ All that was left of a bus when a V-1 exploded in the street at Aldwych.

▶ His face bloodied from a head wound, a middle-aged man is helped out of a blast-shattered building at Aldwych. Twenty-five people were killed in this incident.

◀ The balloon barrage accounted for nearly 300 flying-bombs and at no little risk to the operators as the missiles often fell close to the balloon site. The point of destruction can be seen in the middle of the meadow to the right of the balloon whose cable the V-1 fouled. The blast all but demolished an old barn. The RAF man in the foreground is collecting debris.

◀ Probably one of the most horrific incidents of the V-1 bombardment occurred on Sunday, 18 June 1944 when a service for the Guards was in progress in the Royal Military Chapel at Wellington Barracks. A direct hit killed 119 people and seriously injured 102. This photograph was taken some days later.

some indication that the subterfuge of only publishing casualty lists for West London boroughs paid off in that, believing the V-2s were overshooting, the Germans shortened the range although, unfortunately, not sufficiently for eastern boroughs to escape. Like the V-1, the V-2 was intended to destroy by blast and this they certainly did. While they might come at any time of night or day their arrival was not forewarned by any sound; the first one heard was the distinctive double crack of the explosion – if you were fortunate enough not to be where the missile struck. There was no warning siren because their coming was undetected. But on clear mornings people on the Essex and Suffolk coasts could quite clearly see the exhaust trail left as the rocket climbed to the stratosphere from The Hague area. A few rockets were apparently aimed at Norwich but were widely scattered. V-2s claimed the lives of 2,855 people and seriously injured 6,268.

Meanwhile the air launching of flying-bombs had taken a new turn. In the early morning of 5 September 1944, Heinkels operating over the North Sea began to release V-1s towards the East Anglian coast, a ploy which continued sporadically until the end of March 1945. The launch aircraft suffered severely from interceptions from RAF fighter patrols and spread their launch areas up and down the east coast with Midland and northern cities the intended targets in some cases. In effect the 800 or so V-1s delivered by this method were random shots and mostly came to earth at widely separated locations over the Midlands and eastern England from London to Newcastle. Nevertheless, in total the V-weapons took some 9,000 lives and wounded about 24,000 people. The last Luftwaffe aircraft to carry out offensive action over the United Kingdom came on the night of 21 March, a dozen directing their attention to airfields in the eastern counties.

▲ The extent of the flying-bomb campaign and the success of the defences can be gauged from this wall chart in Churchill's underground War Room. The 3rd of August is pointed out as the date of the highest number of launches, a bad weather day which limited fighter interception.

◄ Rocket propulsion unit of a V-2 lying on an old Blitz site at Limehouse in March 1945.

AFTER THE ALLIED BREAKOUT and sweeping advances in France during the summer of 1944 there was some relaxation of blackout regulations, with subdued lighting being allowed in the streets and at busy road junctions. A programme of replacing road signs and place names had been under way for some months but was not completed until peace returned. Many armchair observers on the Home Front forecast Germany's demise before the end of the year, but this was not to be. Checked at the Rhine, the Allied armies endured a particularly hard winter, repulsing the Wehrmacht's final counter-offensive in the west.

By the spring of 1945 peace, at last, seemed just around the corner. The RAF and US bombers continued their massive aerial bombardment of German targets and on 24 March many people in the south-east watched a force of gliders and their aerial tugs set out for the airborne crossings of the Rhine, the last hurdle. The Third Reich reeled and by late April the British-based bombers set out no more

▲ Twelve-year-old Jean Devereux and her mother examine a Christmas gift from her father serving in Italy. It was made available through the YMCA scheme to obtain and deliver presents for men serving overseas, some 20,000 being handled at Christmas 1944. Trooper Devereux's photograph is on the sideboard.

▶ Buckingham Palace illuminated on the night of VE-Day, 8 May 1945, as crowds packed the area around the Victoria Memorial.

with their lethal loads. At long last the bombardment of Britain was over too, although there were those who expected some last-minute catastrophic act of revenge to be ordered by Hitler. But news soon came that Hitler was dead and 8 May 1945 was officially proclaimed as Victory in Europe Day – VE Day. There were street parties, bonfires, improvised fireworks and dazzling illuminations of the kind so long denied and not known by the very young.

But it was not all over, there was still Japan to defeat and troopships still sailed out of Liverpool bound for the Far East. VE Day brought no lightening in the burden of rationing, in fact some rations were further reduced in the summer of 1945. Japan's defeat was only a matter of time and already war factories could be returned to more peaceful production and a start made on demobilizing nearly five million men and women. A distraction, or so it seemed to many Britons, was the disbandment of Churchill's National coalition government by elections for a new government on party lines. The June result reflected the political awareness that had developed over the past few years. The Labour party had a landslide victory but those who expected the more extreme parties of the left to gain prominence were disappointed. The electorate, conservative by nature, identified more with the solid working class image of labour than with the intellectual socialists of the Common Wealth and Communist parties.

Clement Attlee replaced Churchill as Prime Minister and many of the well-known names in government disappeared from office. Lord Woolton, the popular Minister of Food – despite his vegetable-based Woolton Pie that did not suit wartime palates; the good-looking Anthony Eden, Foreign Secretary; Sir John Anderson, Chancellor of the Exchequer, who in earlier office introduced the garden shelter named after him. Equally well-known stalwarts of the coalition cabinet who, as labour politicians, now served in the new government, were the redoubtable Ernest Bevin, former Minister of Labour and Herbert Morrison who, as Churchill's Home Secretary, had issued the table shelter that took his name.

The new government came to power as Japan's defeat appeared to be imminent. The dropping of the two atomic bombs hastened the latter event and surrender was forthcoming on 14 August. Next day Britain celebrated the war's end, VJ Day.

Compared with the millions of fatalities incurred by Germany, Japan and Russia, the United Kingdom's sacrifice was less severe. The dead totalled 355,000 souls of whom 60,000 were civilians killed on the Home Front and 30,000 merchant seamen. The armed services fatalities were just over 264,000, and of those RAF Bomber Command shouldered the heaviest portion of losses incurred in any single campaign, 55,000.* Neither did Britain emerge with her industry and cities laid waste to the degree suffered by the defeated nations. In other respects fighting the Second World War had seen the demise of Great Britain as a world power and left the nation near bankrupt. For many of the men and women in the street the relief of victory was tinged with incredulity. As one summed it up: 'For all our bloody muddling, we actually made it.'

*British casualty figures for the Second World War vary considerably according to the source one uses. Those presented here are taken from Professor Andrew Calder's *A People's War* (London, 1969), and are considered to be fairly accurate.

The unknown circumstances surrounding a loved one reported killed in action or on active service often haunted next-of-kin: the hope that death had been instantaneous; the fear, prolonged suffering.

At a summer evening tennis party soon after hostilities had ceased, a woman guest, tired of watching her husband play, went to sit in her host's house. As she entered the lounge a young man was playing the piano. When he had finished the piece the woman complimented him on his talent and a conversation ensued. The pianist mentioned that he had played at station concerts while in the RAF and the woman revealed that her son had been killed in a flying accident. Condolences were offered and acknowledged, with the woman saying that while she had come to terms with her son's death she could not extinguish the fear that he might have burned. The pianist sympathized and asked where her son had been serving. On being told South Africa and the name of the airfield, he asked the deceased's name. In response to the answer he said, consolingly: 'This is the most amazing coincidence. I was your son's flying instructor. You can banish your fears of his having burnt to death because I can tell you exactly what happened. He made a heavy landing in a Tiger Moth trainer and was found dead in the cockpit with a broken neck. I remember it well because it was such an extraordinary thing to happen.'

▲Victory Parade: 8 May 1945. The Australian army contingent marches past the saluting stand in the Mall. Standing to the left of the royal party (right of photograph) are Attlee, Churchill, and Field Marshal Smuts. On the other side are the British service chiefs, Sir Dudley Pound, Sir Alan Brooke and Sir Charles Portall.

▶These people living at 'The Laurels' had good reason to hang out the bunting. They lived in German-occupied Guernsey.

▶ Shades of things to come. This Volkswagen Beetle of which the first model appeared in 1938 sponsored by Hitler as the People's Car, caused a great amount of interest when it appeared in Oxford Street in the summer of 1945, having been brought from Germany for an exhibition.

▶ The price. Artificial limb factory at the Queen Mary Hospital, Roehampton. There were plenty of takers.

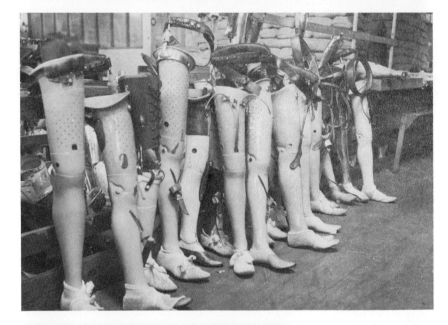

▶ Demob! Those with long service and priority needs were immediately eligible for release. RSM Charles Stilwell of Farnham, Surrey, joined the army in 1914 and had 31 years' continuous service. One of the first men to be demobilized, he is seen being measured for a civilian suit at the Olympia Clothing Depot. 'Civvy Street' next stop!